Contents

UNIT 1

Present tenses

PRESENT SIMPLE (1)

FORM

I / You / We / They **work**.
He / She / It **works**.

I / You / We / They **do** not **work**.
He / She / It **does** not **work**.

Do I / you / we / they **work**?
Does he / she / it **work**?

USES

1 Presenting factual information, e.g. about company activities

Our company **employs** over 100,000 people, **operates** in many overseas markets and **offers** a wide range of hi-tech products for the 21st century.

2 Actions and situations which are generally true

Altadis **belongs to** the Imperial Tobacco group.

High taxation **discourages** investment.

We **sell** our products into many markets.

A good brand **guarantees** a certain level of quality to customers.

British wines usually **have** a sweet taste.

Competition **brings out** the best in products and the worst in people.

3 Verbs used only in the present simple

There are a number of verbs which are almost always used in the present simple and not with *-ing*. These verbs usually refer to:

mental states: believe doubt forget imagine know realise recognise regret remember suppose think understand

liking and disliking: admire dislike hate like love want wish

possession: belong to contain have include own possess

appearance: appear look like resemble seem

being: be consist of depend exist

perception: hear see smell taste

4 Saying how often you or other people do things

We usually use the present simple with frequency adverbs:

I *never* **smoke** at work.

He **plays** golf *every Sunday morning*.

I *often* **take** files home at the weekend.

When she **gets** to the office, she *always* **checks** her e-mail first.

PRACTICE

A Mission statements

A mission statement talks in general terms about a company's overall policies and objectives. Complete the two mission statements with the correct form of these verbs. The first one has been done for you in both cases.

~~admit~~	introduce	lead	welcome	mean	work
depend	improve	stay	come	spend	

Restless? Yes. Dissatisfied? True. We cheerfully ....admit.... it. We always .... [1] change and continuous improvement. Today consumers .... [2] more than $25 billion a year on our products. We .... [3] – or .... [4] a very close second – in all our business segments, which .... [5] that vigorous growth .... [6] on our own imagination, commitment and skill. So we regularly .... [7] new products, ... [8] distribution channels and .... [9] round the clock to be more efficient. Most of all, we .... [10] absolutely and unequivocally 100% geared towards the customer, who's definitely number one in our book!

~~believe~~	strive	cultivate	deliver	enable	
help	give	endeavour	acknowledge	foster	

Eastman Kodak Company ....believes.... that a diverse group of highly skilled people, in an organizational culture which .... [11] them to apply their collective talents to shared objectives, ... [12] the greatest value to customers and shareowners alike. The company and its employees .... [13] to support an inclusive Kodak culture that .... [14] unique thinking in the context of teamwork and common business goals.

Kodak .... [15] to provide a flexible, supportive work environment that .... [16] employees as partners in the business and community. To this end, it .... [17] employees access to a multitude of work/life resources and .... [18] programs that .... [19] individuals balance their commitment to meeting business needs with their personal, family, and community responsibilities.

B General truths

Complete the sayings appropriately with these verbs.

buy	believe (x2)	tend	promise	say	put	mean	talk

1 'Every time we .... a foreign car we .... someone else out of work.' (Woodrow Wyatt)

2 'Money .... they .... All it ever said to me was "Goodbye".' (Cary Grant)

3 'Democracy .... government by discussion, but it is only effective if you can stop people talking.' (Clement Attlee, British Prime Minister)

4 'Politicians are the same all over. They .... to build a bridge even where there is no river.' (Khrushchev)

5 'In a hierarchy every employee .... to rise to his level of incompetence.' (Laurence J. Peter)

6 'Not all Germans .... in God, but they .... in the Bundesbank.' (Jacques Delors)

PRESENT SIMPLE (2)

USES

5 Asking for and giving directions and instructions

'How do I **get** to your office?'

'You **turn** left after the station, **cross** the bridge and it's the second building on your right.'

Place the CD in the drive and **click** on the icon.

6 Talking about timetables and scheduled events

The bus **leaves** at 8.35 tomorrow morning.

The exhibition **opens** on 25 January.

The legislation **comes** into force on 1 January.

These are seen as fixed and the speaker is unlikely to be able to influence them.

➡ *Future 2.5* page 30

7 Providing a summary or abstract at the beginning of a report

The first section of this report **provides** introductory comments, **focuses** on important new developments and **highlights** some of our operations outside the United States. The second section **analyses** the results for the group as a whole. The final two sections **address** our consolidated cash flows and financial condition. The report **concludes** by pointing out the need for further investment if the group is to continue its expansion policy.

8 Newspaper headlines

The use of the present simple creates a sense of dramatic impact.

MARKETS TUMBLE AS INVESTORS TAKE PROFITS

Shortages force up food prices

Russia doubles tea import duties

Unilever sells coffee operations

BANK REGULATOR BLOCKS MERGER

WPP WARNS ON TAX PLANS

9 Doing by saying

We use the present simple with certain verbs which say what their function is. When we say them, we 'perform' the action. For example, saying '**I promise** to meet you at the airport' is making a promise. Other examples include:

I **resign**!

I **declare** this meeting open.

I **admit** I was wrong.

I **apologise**.

I **demand** to see the manager.

I **advise** you to look again at our proposal.

PRACTICE

A A travel booking

Complete the dialogue about travel arrangements with the correct form of the verbs in brackets.

Traveller Hello, I ....[1] (need) to go to London next Friday and come back on the same day. I've a meeting which ....[2] (start) at 10 o'clock.

Agent .... you ....[3] (want) to fly or take the train?

Traveller That ....[4] (depend) on the price. How much .... it ....[5] (cost)?

Agent The train ....[6] (be) cheaper and ....[7] (get) you right into the centre of London. It ....[8] (take) just two and a quarter hours.

Traveller OK, that's fine. What about times?

Agent Well, Eurostar ....[9] (leave) Paris at 7.13 and ....[10] (arrive) in London at 8.28 local time.

Traveller What time .... I ....[11] (have to) check in?

Agent Not later than 30 minutes before departure.

Traveller OK. How .... I ....[12] (make) a reservation?

B A summary of a report

Complete the introduction to the report with these verbs.

highlight	recommend	focus	call for	provide

This report ....[1] on the employment of women and children in a number of emerging nations. In particular, it ....[2] the conditions endured by thousands of workers in places where child labour, poverty wages and health risks are endemic. Each chapter ....[3] an analysis of the situation on a country-by-country basis.

The report ....[4] that retailers should lay down tough rules to make sure overseas suppliers pay sufficient wages to meet basic needs. It also ....[5] companies to draw up a code of conduct and employ inspectors to make manufacturers keep to it.

C Headlines

Match the beginnings and ends of the headlines.

1 FORD SEEKS TO CUT
2 STOCKMARKETS SLIP
3 SÃO PAULO DEBT CRISIS
4 CHINA RENEWS ATTACK
5 PESSIMISTS FORESEE
6 UNDERWATER VENTURE NEEDS

a) SENDS OUT SHOCK WAVES
b) DEATH OF FULL EMPLOYMENT
c) ON US TECHNOLOGY REPORT
d) BACKING TO STAY AFLOAT
e) AS DOLLAR FALLS AGAINST YEN
f) $1bn IN COSTS

PRESENT CONTINUOUS (1)

FORM

I **am working**.
You / We / They **are working**.
He / She / It **is working**.

I **am** not **working**.
You / We / They **are** not **working**.
He / She / It **is** not **working**.

Am I **working**?
Are you / we / they **working**?
Is he / she / it **working**?

USES

1 Talking about an event in progress at the moment of speaking

'What **are** you **doing**?' '**I'm trying** to find a file.'

I'm afraid Mr Bansall can't see you right now. He**'s interviewing** someone.

We also often use the continuous with verbs of movement when the action has just started:

I**'m leaving**. Can you tell Rosemary I'll see her tomorrow?

'Can I speak to John?' 'Sorry, he's out. No, hold on, he**'s** just **coming** down the corridor.'

2 Describing current situations and ongoing projects

The time reference is at and around 'now', before and after the situations referred to. But the situation may not be in progress literally at the exact moment of speaking.

We**'re waiting** for permission to go ahead with the project.

Big Japanese companies **are thinking** again about uniform pay systems.

My boss **is dealing** with your enquiry but you won't get a rapid answer.

3 Describing temporary situations

When the present continuous is used in this way, the situation described will not last permanently.

They**'re staying** at the Crillon Hotel until the end of the week.

He**'s working** in Libya on a fixed-term contract.

They **are offering** a 20% discount for the duration of the trade fair.

PRACTICE

A Events in progress

Look at the pictures and decide what is happening in each one.

1 

2 

3 

4 

5 

6 

B News in brief

Read the extracts about projects that various companies are currently involved in. Match the extracts in column A with those in column B.

A

1 Qatar Telecom intends to pursue its rapid expansion policy to achieve its goal of becoming one of the world's top 20 telecommunications companies.

2 'IBM in Europe chooses schools with the technology to teach collaboration,' writes Della Bradshaw.

3 Showa Shell Sekiyu and Cosmo Oil are stepping up plans to cut costs and improve cash flow.

4 The New Zealand government has decided to sell the country's second biggest electricity generator.

5 Strong sales of BlackBerry smartphones helped Research in Motion report a 72% increase in second-quarter net income.

B

a) The chief reforms are the elimination of 900 jobs and the reduction of sales, general and administrative expenses.

b) The firm is opting for external management training in a big way and is using its purchasing power to push the business schools involved into adopting the very latest technology to deliver their courses.

c) The firm will launch at least three new handsets before the end of the year.

d) Its chairperson said, 'Whenever we see an opportunity, we'll go ahead aggressively.'

e) It is seeking commercial advisers for the sale of Contact Energy, which produces 27% of the country's energy supply.

C Temporary situations

Complete the sentences appropriately.

1 There are no trains this week because of the strike so ...
2 Her boss is off sick at the moment so ...
3 We've got builders in our house so ...
4 There are rumours of a devaluation so ...

PRESENT CONTINUOUS (2)

USES

4 Changing, developing situations

We use the present continuous to describe changes which have not yet finished:

The number of people using Facebook **is growing**.

The Amazon rainforest **is disappearing** at an alarming rate.

Consumers in the industrialised world **are becoming** increasingly concerned with healthy living.

5 Personal arrangements and plans

We use the present continuous to refer to future time when talking about arrangements and fixed plans made before the time of speaking. We often use a time expression unless we are sure that the other person knows we are talking about the future:

I**'m seeing** Mr Poorhassan next weekend.

I**'m taking** the client to the best restaurant in town.

She's got a new job so she**'s leaving** the firm in October.

We also use the present continuous with verbs of movement to talk about actions which are just beginning:

It's 1 o'clock. I**'m going** to the canteen for lunch. **Are** you **coming**?

6 Talking about repeated actions

His daughter **is taking** driving lessons.

His wife **is** always **telling** him not to work so hard.

We **are** constantly **monitoring** our products for quality.

If we describe repeated situations using the present continuous with *always*, the situation is often unplanned. Compare:

I always **meet** Marilyn in the car park. (planned in advance)

I**'m** always **meeting** Marilyn in the car park. (by chance)

PRACTICE

A Changes

Write about any changes the government of your country is currently making in the following sectors, as in the example.

EXAMPLE: business and finance *The government is setting up new enterprise schemes.*

1 the environment ....

2 taxation ....

3 the law ....

4 transportation ....

5 education ....

6 health ....

B Arrangements

Complete the dialogue appropriately with verbs in the present continuous.

A Are you free next Wednesday?

B No, sorry. I'm afraid I ....[1].

A Well, I can't make it on Thursday so what about Friday?

B In the morning I ....[2] but in the afternoon I ....[3] anything special.

A Fine, that's OK by me.

C Present simple or present continuous?

Which of these ideas do you associate with the present simple (PS) and which with the present continuous (PC)?

.... 1 regular activities

.... 2 temporary situations

.... 3 fixed timetables

.... 4 giving instructions

.... 5 an event in progress

.... 6 permanent and factual situations

.... 7 a present arrangement for the future

.... 8 mental states

.... 9 trends and changing situations

.... 10 doing by saying

Which sentence a–j corresponds to each of 1–10 above?

a) I'm replacing Bill because he's off sick.

b) The scheduled flight leaves next Monday at 8.15 from JFK.

c) The technician is mending the photocopier so you can't use it right now.

d) I'm seeing Bill Sykes tomorrow afternoon. I've got it in my diary.

e) The conference room measures 164 square metres.

f) I admit there has been a mistake.

g) I understand they have gone bankrupt.

h) Enter PIN number, select menu, choose language, press OK.

i) With the Internet the world is getting smaller.

j) We have a planning meeting once a month.

UNIT 2

Past tenses

PAST SIMPLE

FORM

I / You / He / She / It / We / They **worked**.
I / You / He / She / It / We / They **did** not **work**.
Did I / you / he / she / it / we / they **work**?

I / He / She / It **was** late.
You / We / They **were** late.
Was I / he / she / it late?
Were you / we / they late?

USES

1 Talking about completed actions that happened in the past

Alexander Graham Bell **invented** the telephone.

'**Did** you read the contract?' 'Yes, and I **sent** it back to the legal department.'

2 Referring to a definite moment or period in the past

I **met** the president *yesterday*.

I **spoke** to them *an hour ago*.

Google Inc. **launched** its web browser Google Chrome™ *in 2008*.

The standard of living in Europe **went up** *during the 1960s*.

Did you **discuss** the problem *at last week's meeting*?

3 Describing something, e.g. the history of a company

Two brothers, Will Keith Kellogg and Dr John Harvey Kellogg, **founded** the Battle Creek Toasted Corn Flake Company on February 19, 1906, in the belief that the public **needed** a lighter, healthier breakfast cereal. In 1922 the firm **changed** its name to the Kellogg Company.

To help consumers distinguish Kellogg's Corn Flakes® from the products of the 42 other cereal companies in Battle Creek, Michigan, W.K. **put** his signature on each package, saying that these Corn Flakes **were** the "The Original."

During the Great Depression of the 1930s, the firm **made** an original move. Instead of cutting back, it **doubled** advertising spending and Kellogg cereal sales **improved**. Employees **kept** their jobs, working 30 hours a week instead of 40. Some of the workers **earned** their paychecks by developing a 10-acre park on the Battle Creek plant grounds.

4 In reports, e.g. a company's annual report

We use the past simple in annual reports when they refer back to the previous year's trading:

Last year **was** a tough year for our group. On the one hand, we **earned** more than a billion dollars, we **generated** record cash flow and many of our businesses **posted** big gains in sales, profit and market share. On the other hand, our total earnings **declined**, our overseas subsidiaries **experienced** major problems and our US production facilities **underperformed**.

PRACTICE

A Important firsts

What made these people famous? Write true sentences and change the form of the verb.

EXAMPLE: John Logie Baird gave the first public demonstration of television in 1926.

1	John Logie Baird	invent	the first flight in 1903.
2	The Wright brothers	discover	radium in 1902.
3	Neil Armstrong	make	the first commercial sewing machine in 1851.
4	Pierre and Marie Curie	patent	the first public demonstration of television in 1926.
5	Gutenberg	give	the printing press in 1434.
6	Isaac Singer	land	on the surface of the moon in 1969.

B The Dell story

Complete each paragraph with the verbs in the boxes.

have say begin introduce open

In 1984 Michael Dell .... [1] his computer business at the University of Texas in Austin. In 1986 his company .... [2] the 286-12 machine, which the magazine *PC Week* .... [3] 'may become the next industry benchmark'. The following year he .... [4] an office in the United Kingdom and soon .... [5] offices in 33 countries.

total decide employ run go

In the summer of 1988, Dell .... [6] public. By now the firm .... [7] 650 people and sales .... [8] over $159 million. Then two years later employees .... [9] to celebrate 1 April by hanging a giant inflatable gorilla outside company headquarters, the first of many publicity stunts. On another occasion the CEO .... [10] around a stadium carrying the Olympic torch.

become expand launch overtake stay step down win

In 1991 Dell .... [11] its first notebook PC and in the same year .... [12] the first PC maker to install applications software free for its clients. The company .... [13] at a rapid rate with subsidiaries opening in Belgium, Finland, Luxembourg, Norway and Spain. In 1999 Dell .... [14] Compaq to become the largest seller of PCs in the United States with $25 billion in revenue reported in January 2000. On 4 March 2004, Michael Dell .... [15] as CEO but .... [16] on as chairman of the board. The company is now the leading PC provider in the US and second worldwide. In 2007 Dell .... [17] more than 200 product awards.

C An annual report

Complete the extract with these verbs. There are more verbs than necessary.

delay choose improve give make stabilise hinder

Last year the international situation in the hydrocarbons industry .... [1] to some extent. However, the volatile foreign exchange rates .... [2] currency management more difficult and relatively weak demand .... [3] expansion projects. We therefore .... [4] to focus our efforts on specific opportunities where our know-how .... [5] us a technical advantage over particularly aggressive competition. As a result, we propose doubling our dividend against a background of stronger cash position and balance sheet ratios.

PAST CONTINUOUS

FORM

I **was working**.
You / We / They **were working**.
He / She / It **was working**.

I **was** not **working**.
You / We / They **were** not **working**.
He / She / It **was** not **working**.

Was I **working**?
Were you / we / they **working**?
Was he / she / it **working**?

USES

1 Emphasising the duration or continuity of a past event

He **was working** on the report all day long.

During the 1990s computer scientists **were trying** to deal with the millennium bug.

2 Describing a background event

We use the past continuous to describe an event which was in progress when it was interrupted by another one. The second, shorter event, is in the past simple:

I **was** just **leaving** the office when he **arrived**.

We **were talking** about safety procedures when the fire alarm **went off**.

3 For repeated events

He **was visiting** clients all last week and didn't come into the office. (a number of different clients)

Last month we **were having** a lot of problems with the production line. (a number of different problems)

However, the past continuous is *not* normally used for the same action which is repeated or for habitual past actions:

The production line **stopped** five times yesterday. (NOT *was stopping)

When I was at business school, we often **worked** on case studies. (NOT *were working on)

4 Making polite requests

I **was wondering** if you could give me a lift.

There is no idea of past time here. The past verb form creates social 'distance' and makes the request less direct and therefore more polite.

5 For events planned in the past which did not take place

I **was planning** to visit the exhibition but I went to the football match instead.

She **was going** to phone them yesterday but didn't have the time.

PRACTICE

A The reasons why

Use the words in the box to give explanations for the following events. The first one has been done for you.

~~funds~~	plummet	the president	suffer	the fire bell	~~run out~~
my work	complain	their value	ring	customers	speak

1 We scrapped the project because funds were running out.
2 They evacuated the building because ....
3 He sold his shares quickly because ....
4 He didn't wish to interrupt because ....
5 I cut down on drinking because ....
6 We were forced to withdraw the model because ....

B Jeff Bezos

Complete the passage with these sentences.

a) 'We weren't betting on the Internet,' his mother has said. 'We were betting on Jeff.'
b) Amazon was selling books in all 50 American states and 45 foreign countries.
c) was building a network to conduct international trade.
d) Internet use was increasing by 2,300 per cent a year.
e) and was looking forward to a bright career in finance
f) While he was working at Shaw,

After graduation from Princeton University, Jeff Bezos found employment on Wall Street, where computer science was increasingly in demand to study market trends. His first job was with Fitel, a start-up company that ....[1]

He then moved to D. E. Shaw, a firm specialising in the application of computer science to the stock market. ....[2] Jeff met his wife, Mackenzie, also a Princeton graduate. He rose quickly to become a senior Vice President ....[3] when he made a discovery that changed his life and the course of business history.

In 1994 there was still no internet commerce to speak of. But one day that spring, he discovered that ....[4] He saw an opportunity for a new sphere of commerce and immediately began considering the possibilities.

He and his wife created an internet site and asked 300 friends and acquaintances to test it. It worked perfectly across different computer platforms. On July 16, 1995, Bezos opened his site to the world and asked his 300 testers to spread the word. Very soon, and with no advertising, ...[5]

The company went public in 1997 and Jeff told his investors there was a 70 per cent chance they would lose their entire investment. His parents also signed on for $300,000, a substantial portion of their life savings. ....[6] By the end of the decade, as six per cent owners of Amazon.com, they were billionaires.

PAST PERFECT SIMPLE

FORM I / You / He / She / It/ We / They **had worked**. **Had** I / you / he / she / it/ we / they **worked**?
I / You / He / She / It / We / They **had** not **worked**.

USES

1 Talking about events that happened before other events

In the extract below the events in bold type refer to an earlier past:

had climbed into the dryer = before the accident

his employer had not given him proper training = before the accident

had been an unlawful killing = before the trial

had died = before the trial

Paul Bennett was killed after he **had climbed** into a giant industrial tumble dryer to free a piece of cloth trapped inside. The machine started accidentally and he was spun to death at a heat of 43°C. It became evident that his employer **had not given** him proper training and a jury decided that there **had been** an 'unlawful killing' – it was satisfied beyond reasonable doubt that Mr Bennett **had died** as a result of manslaughter.

2 With *I wish*, *If only* and *I'd rather*

We use the past perfect to talk about events that did not happen:

I wish I **had been** more interested in English at school.

If only I **had bought** those shares; they've gone up 27%.

I'd rather he**'d asked** me before taking my car.

In the negative, the sentence expresses a regret for events that did take place:

He wishes he **hadn't left** his previous job. (but he did)

3 Emphasising the recent nature and/or duration of actions

If we want to focus on continuous activity taking place in an earlier past, we use the continuous form:

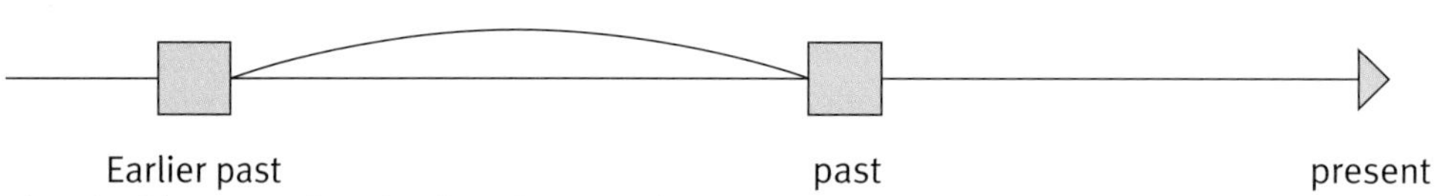

They **had been testing** the drug for years before it came onto the market.

She had to take a break because she**'d been working** far too hard.

PRACTICE

A Susan George's CV

Read the CV and complete the sentences about Susan George with these verbs.

develop	market	be	obtain	spend

1 Before she went to Lancaster University, Susan .... three A levels.
2 Before she got her degree in biochemistry, she .... three years in Lancaster.
3 Before she joined Fisons, she .... on a marketing course.
4 Before she worked at Rootes AgriTec, she .... disease-resistant rice plants.
5 Before she became a product manager at Boots, she .... remedies for Alzheimer's disease.

NAME: Susan Mary GEORGE
ADDRESS: 31 Whitstable Road, Canterbury, Kent CT6 W33
DATE OF BIRTH: 9.7.83

QUALIFICATIONS:

Simon Langton Grammar School 2001
GCE 'A' Levels: Maths (Grade B), Biology (Grade B),Chemistry (Grade C)

Lancaster University 2001–2004
BSc 2.1 Biochemistry

Keele Management College 2005
Eight-week course in marketing

WORK EXPERIENCE:

2005–2007 Fisons Pharmaceutical Products
Research assistant responsible for the development of genetically modified disease-resistant rice plants.

2007–2009 Rootes AgriTec
Junior executive responsible to Product Manager for commercialising new remedies for Alzheimer's disease.

2009–present Boots
Product Manager, responsible for over-the-counter medicines.

B Regrets

Susan has been relatively successful, but things did not always turn out as she had hoped. Complete the sentences with the correct form of the verbs in brackets.

1 She wishes she .... (get) better 'A' level grades.
2 She wishes she .... (obtain) a distinction at degree level.
3 She wishes she .... (do) a doctorate.
4 She wishes the marketing course .... (last) longer than eight weeks.

PAST PERFECT CONTINUOUS

FORM I / You / He / She / It / We / They **had been working**. **Had** I / you / he / she / it / we / they **been working**?
I / You / He / She / It / We / They **had** not **been working**.

USES

1 Talking about events that happened before other events

Like the past perfect simple (see page 18), the past perfect continuous looks back to an event that took place before another past event.

The main difference is that the continuous form emphasises the duration of the first event.

So we normally use the continuous with an expression indicating how long: *for over an hour, for a long time, since 1999*, etc.

I**'d been trying** to get through *for over an hour* before someone answered the phone.

He**'d been thinking** of going abroad *for a long time* and then he got a post in Singapore.

Before they closed down the subsidiary, it **had been losing** money *ever since it was set up*.

2 Finished and unfinished activities

Compare:

a) When I last saw her, she**'d been planning** a new sales strategy.

b) When I last saw her, she**'d planned** a new sales strategy.

In sentence a) the planning may or may not have been completed; we don't know whether the new sales strategy was abandoned or not.

In sentence b) it is clear that the planning had reached an end-point.

Note that we do not use the continuous form with verbs describing permanent states, perception, etc. (For a list see Present simple (1) on page 6.) In such cases we use the past perfect simple.

The man who said there was no future in computers **hadn't understood** their significance.

NOT *The man who said there was no future in computers hadn't been understanding their significance.

PRACTICE

A Previous and subsequent events

Complete the sentences with the past perfect simple or continuous.

1 My flight from Sydney arrived late because there .... (be) a bomb alert before the plane took off. When we finally left, we .... (wait) for over five hours.

2 I .... (work) hard all year so I felt I needed a rest.

3 I .... (see) the designs before they went on show but they .... (not impress) me.

4 When I bought my BIP shares, their value .... (fall) for some time.

5 The merchant bank didn't know that one of their traders .... (hide) huge losses.

6 The employee was dismissed because he .... (steal) company property ever since he was taken on.

7 It took me twenty minutes to realise I .... (look) in the wrong file.

B Marcel Bich

Read the extract about Marcel Bich's early career and complete the sentences below. If it is not possible to use the past perfect continuous, use the simple form.

Marcel Bich set up in business in 1949 and created France's most successful company and its third best-known brand after Dior and Chanel.

He was educated in Italy as a child, followed by two years at the Lycée Français in Madrid. He completed his secondary education in Bordeaux, where he received the nickname 'Baron' – a title that he carried for the rest of his life. At 18, he began selling torches door-to-door and later said that this experience was critical to his entrepreneurial success.

At university he studied mathematics and philosophy and after graduation began work as a production manager for an office machine company. He then joined Stephens, a large French pen manufacturer, as a production executive, but the Second World War interrupted his career. When the war was over, he decided he wanted to set up on his own.

1 Before he died, he .... (create) France's most successful company.

2 Before going to Bordeaux, he .... (study) in Italy and Spain.

3 Before he went to university, he .... (sell) torches door-to-door.

4 Prior to becoming a production manager, he .... (study) maths and philosophy.

5 Before the Second World War broke out, he .... (work) for Stephens as a production executive.

UNIT 3

Combining past and present

PRESENT PERFECT SIMPLE (1)

FORM

I / You / We / They **have worked**.
He / She / It **has worked**.

I / You / We / They **have** not **worked**.
He /She / It **has** not **worked**.

Have I / you / we / they **worked**?
Has he / she / it **worked**?

USES

1 Talking about present results of past actions

In this extract, the impact of information technology over the last few years is described in terms of its present significance:

IT **has shaken up** company structures just as much as external markets, says Vanessa Houlder.

To enthusiasts, information technology is forging a productivity revolution. It **has changed** not just the nature of markets and competition. Inside companies, it **has** also **changed** behaviour. It **has broken down** the barriers of geography and time. It **has flattened** organisational structures, eliminating vast numbers of jobs, while making others more demanding and effective.

2 Announcing news

The use of the present perfect simple focuses on current relevance:

Our fax number **has changed**.

We**'ve** just **lowered** our prices.

They **have updated** their website.

The government **has announced** a decrease in corporation tax.

The transport minister **has launched** a plan to improve safety and security.

3 With time adverbs

We use the present perfect simple to say how long a situation that began in the past has lasted up to the moment of speaking:

He**'s been** vice-president *for* ten years.

He**'s had** the same job *since* 2006.

She**'s** *always* **been** a creative person.

PRACTICE

A India and China

This is part of a discussion between Martin Wolf, chief economics columnist on the *Financial Times*, and Quentin Peel, international affairs commentator on the *Financial Times*, about China and India. Read the dialogue and choose between the past simple and present perfect. The first one has been done for you.

QP China *has always been* / ~~*was always*~~ a great source of fascination but now it is China and India. *Have we been* / *Were we* [1] guilty of ignoring India for too long?

MW Clearly, China *has had* / *had* [2] an enormous impact on the world economy. But India is opening and in some ways India is where China *has been* / *was* [3] ten to fifteen years ago.

QP In what ways *has India changed* / *did India change*[4]?

MW Well, the important reforms which *have taken place* / *took place* [5] in June 1991 at the time of the balance of payments crisis *have had* / *had* [6] a long-term effect. It *has taken* / *took* [7] them a long time since the 1980s to transform the economy and to build the confidence that Indian business people and overseas investors need.

QP And what about the key differences between India and China?

MW What is interesting is that they *have remained* / *remained* [8] remarkably different in their development. China is the classic east-Asian export-led industrialised economy flooding the world with products we *have previously associated* / *previously associated* [9] with Japan and South Korea. On the other hand, in India the service sector is dominant and in particular IT service exports *have been* / *were* [10] exceptionally important.

QP Is there any reason for this?

MW I think the intellectual services that India *has specialised* / *specialised* [11] in are the perfect export industry for Brahmins. India *has always had* / *always had* [12] a powerful tradition of scholars, mathematicians and scientists and this area fits them perfectly. India *has never chosen* / *never chose* [13] the route of massive industrialisation. On the contrary it *has pursued* / *pursued* [14] policies that actively discouraged it.

FT

B Market news in brief

These announcements were read out today during a radio programme called *Business in Action*. Complete each one with these verbs in either the past simple or the present perfect.

issue	launch (x2)	announce	slump

Cable & Wireless .... [1] its agreement for a £1bn pension fund deal.

Shares in Marks and Spencer, Britain's biggest retailer, ... [2] by more than 10% in the last 24 hours after the firm .... [3] a profits warning.

Asda, the supermarket chain owned by Wal-Mart, ... [4] a non-food arm, Asda Direct, in a bid to grab market share from rivals Tesco and Argos. The website, which offers more than 9,000 products, will be accompanied by a print run of 3m catalogues.

Tesco .... [5] Tesco Direct two years ago and now offers about 12,000 products online and about 7,000 in its catalogue.

PRESENT PERFECT SIMPLE (2)

USES

4 Talking about life experiences

He**'s done** many jobs in his time. He**'s sold** encyclopaedias, he**'s been** a journalist, he**'s worked** in a shoe factory and now he's a trade unionist.

There is no focus here on *when* he did these things in the past. Only the experiences are important.

5 With expressions referring to 'time up to now'

Have you **ever** visited Beijing?	(ever = at any previous time up to now)
I've **never** seen Niagara Falls.	(never = at no previous time up to now)
I've **already** had a word with Bruce.	(already = before now)
Hasn't she decided what to do **yet**?	(yet = until the present time)
We've had a good year **so far**.	(so far = up until now)
We've grown rapidly **over the last few years**.	(= recent years up until now)

See page 14 for the time expressions which are used with the past simple and not the present perfect.

6 After *this is the first / second time*

This is the first time we **have (ever) received** a complaint.

It's only the second time we**'ve met**.

7 Referring to a completed event in the future after *when*, *as soon as*, etc.

I can't make a decision *if* I **haven't received** all the data.

I'll phone you *when* **I've received** confirmation. (OR when I **receive**)

I won't make a decision *until* I **have spoken** to the CEO. (OR until I **speak**)

I'll leave *as soon as* **I've finished**. (OR as soon as I **finish**)

➔ *Future 3.11* page 32

I've been on more headed notepaper than you've had business lunches.

PRACTICE

A Previous experience

Read Christopher Harvey's CV. Ask and answer the questions below using the present perfect or past simple.

EDUCATION

2005–2007 Master's degree in Financial Administration
Project: setting up an import company in Spain

2001–2004 Business Studies, Henley Management School
Project: market survey of perfume sales in France, Spain and Italy

EMPLOYMENT

2009–present Steelcase Strafor (Spain)
Marketing assistant reporting to the marketing director. I managed a dealer development programme involving five other members of staff, created a mail order catalogue sent to 5,000 customers, compiled a database on competing products and planned roadshows for the launch of new products.

2007–2008 American Cyanamid (Spain)
Export assistant in charge of order processing, customs clearance, dealing with delivery delays.

LANGUAGES Spanish: fluent English: fluent

COMPUTER LITERACY Linux, Microsoft Office, QuarkXpress, Photoshop

EXAMPLES:

live abroad?

Has he ever lived abroad? Yes, he has. He lived in Spain for a number of years.

study economics?

Has he ever studied economics? No, he hasn't, but he has studied finance.

1 be in charge of a team?
2 set up a business?
3 have direct sales experience?
4 use Excel?
5 organise exhibitions?
6 deal with export procedures?

B Time words

Sort these words into two categories: *Used with the present perfect* and *Used with the past simple*.

ago yet so far lately since last year over the last two years for the past three weeks yesterday at 3 o'clock since 2007

Choose the correct adverb.

1 I've *yet / already / so far* spoken to Peter about it.
2 We've made a lot of progress *over the past three years / since three years / during three years.*
3 We set up *two years ago / since 2007 / over the last two years.*

PRESENT PERFECT CONTINUOUS

FORM

I / You / We / They **have been working**.
He / She / It **has been working**.

I / You / We / They **have** not **been working**.
He / She / It **has** not **been working**.

Have I / you / we / they been **working**?
Has he / she / it **been working**?

USES

1 Talking about continuous activities

We use the present perfect continuous when the focus is on an extended period of time. The situation or activity started in the past and has been in progress for a period until now.

Exports **have been growing** steadily over the past six months.

Foreign earnings **have been moving** ahead to record levels.

The above situations are incomplete; the present perfect simple, on the other hand, tells us that the action has finished.

Compare:

I**'ve been reading** your proposals.	She**'s been checking** the calculations.	(focus on the activities)
I**'ve read** your proposal.	She**'s checked** the calculations.	(focus on their completion)

2 Talking about the effect of recent events

'Why are your hands so dirty?' 'I**'ve been trying** to repair my car all afternoon.'

'You look tired!' 'I am. I**'ve been working** on the report all day.'

What is important is the present result or evidence of this recent activity – in the first example, his hands are dirty; in the second, he looks tired.

3 Talking about repeated actions

Compare:

Have you **seen** my wife? (I'm looking for her)

Have you **been seeing** my wife? (I suspect you're both having an affair)

But we cannot use *-ing* if we specify the number of occasions or a quantity:

I**'ve been playing** a lot of golf recently.

I**'ve played** golf twice this week. (NOT *I've been playing ...)

I**'ve written** 15 pages today. (NOT *I've been writing ...)

PRACTICE

A Recent activities

Answer these questions with reference to your own situation.

1 What projects have you been working on recently?

2 Who have you been working with?

3 What have you been trying to do but have not yet succeeded in doing?

B The effects of recent events

1 **What explanations could there be for the following?**

a) Thomas always looks worried and in a hurry. He also finds it difficult to sleep at night.

He's been working too hard.

b) There are fewer knives and forks in the canteen than a month ago.

c) Top secret company information often gets reported in the press.

d) A lot of dead fish have been found in the river next to the chemicals plant.

e) Pamela was unable to speak any Spanish on her last trip to Madrid but now she can.

2 **Complete the sentences with the present perfect simple or continuous.**

a) How long (you / wait)? ....

b) I (play) tennis four times this week. ....

c) Look outside. It (rain); the pavement's still wet. ....

d) 'You look tired.' 'I (drive) all day long.' ....

e) I (know) John since we were at school together. ....

f) The government (announce) a drop in unemployment. ....

g) I (read) a book on negotiating skills but I don't think I'll finish it. ....

h) He (work) as a consultant for three different firms in the same sector of activity; I think there's a conflict of interest and he should resign. ....

....

i) He (work) as a consultant for three different firms in the same sector of activity but was fired from the first two. ....

....

j) International phone call rates (fall) for the past two years and the trend shows no sign of reversing.

....

UNIT 4

The future

FUTURE (1)

FORM There are a number of ways of making reference to future time. These include:

present continuous:	I'**m seeing** Kamil tomorrow.
going to:	We'**re going to** discuss the new secret deal.
present simple:	His plane **gets** to Heathrow at 12.45.
will:	It **will** probably arrive late owing to air traffic congestion.
future perfect simple:	I'**ll have arranged** his hotel accommodation by then.
future perfect continuous:	He'**ll be staying** at the Mansion House Hotel.
be + infinitive:	You **are to tell** nobody of our discussions.

USES

1 Talking about plans or arrangements

We can talk about plans using the present continuous:

I'**m meeting** Mr Wong next week. He'**s arriving** on Tuesday.

2 Talking about present intentions

We use *going to* rather than *will* for plans, decisions and firm intentions:

She is **going to** leave in a month's time. (Avoid She will leave ...)

When are you **going to** visit us next? (= When do you intend to ...?)

How much money are you **going to** offer? (= have you decided to offer?)

In general, we prefer a present form when the future event involves some sort of present plan, intention or arrangement. We prefer *will* when we are not focusing on a present idea. Compare:

He'**s taking** early retirement. He'll have a lot more free time. (the decision is already made)

He'**s going to take** early retirement. (present intention / arrangement)

Nobody **will** ever **take** him seriously again. (future situation)

3 Making predictions

To make a prediction we can use either *will* or *going to*:

I'm sure you **will** / **are going to** enjoy your visit to our Head Office.

We use *going to* when there is present external evidence for a future event and *will* when we state our own intuitions:

Look at those clouds – it'**s going to** rain.

I expect he'**ll** want to stay in the best hotel. (I know what kind of person he is)

PRACTICE

A Ambitions

Each of the children has an ambition. What do they intend to be when they grow up?

EXAMPLE: Susan is going to be a pilot.

1 Susan 2 Linda 3 Elizabeth 4 Michael 5 Karen 6 Sean

B Predictions

These questions and answers were published on a *Financial Times* online forum. Match the questions 1–4 with the answers a–d.

1 The global meltdown has affected almost all sectors. Does this mean that doing a Master's degree in Management is money down the drain?

2 Which knowledge set will be most valuable in the coming 20 years?

3 What prospects do you see for postgraduates who are specialised in IT Security and E-commerce?

4 How important is a summer placement when trying to land a full-time post?

a) Companies will be reluctant to give permanent positions in the next two years so recruiters will be keen to assess potential employees' abilities before they take anyone on.

b) These are areas of growing demand but it will really depend on the local job market.

c) Students are going to find recruitment pretty hard but those with a Master's will be better placed than those who only have an undergraduate degree.

d) Commercial agility with the ability to develop business partnerships for profitable growth will be key.

FUTURE (2)

USES

4 Making promises or offers

Will is used to make a commitment for the future:

Could you lend me $50? I**'ll** pay you back tomorrow.

I don't know if I can finish the job by Friday but I**'ll** do my best.

We use *will* (usually contracted to *'ll*) when an offer is made at the moment of speaking:

Are you going? I**'ll** give you a lift to the station if you like.

'I haven't got any means of transport.' 'Don't worry, I**'ll** lend you my car.'

5 Official calendars and schedules

For a future event based on an official calendar or schedule we use the present simple. The event is unlikely to change between now and then.

The train **leaves** from Waterloo at 17.59.

Our next planning meeting **is** on Wednesday.

What time **does** the flight **arrive**?

6 Events completed before a future time

For events that will be finished before a time in the future we use the future perfect simple:

By the time they arrive we **will have gone home**.

At the end of the year we **will have recovered** our initial investment.

7 Events happening as a matter of course

We use the future continuous to describe situations which will arise in the future if things go on as predicted and follow their expected pattern:

No doubt the unions **will be asking** for more money.

She**'ll be retiring** at the end of the year.

Over the next few years average temperatures **will be rising**.

PRACTICE

A Making offers

How could you offer to help in these situations?

1 'It's really hot and stuffy in here.'

2 'I don't understand this English and it needs translating.'

3 'This desk is too heavy. I can't move it.'

4 'Damn! I've missed the last bus.'

5 'I don't know how I'm going to find time to prepare any slides.'

B Schedules

Look at the timetable. Ask questions which elicit the answers below.

Rome → Naples		
Depart	Arrive	Flight No.
09.50	10.45	AZ 1263
11.30	12.25	AZ 1269

Rome → Rimini		
Depart	Arrive	Flight No.
12.00	13.00	AZ 7872
17.50	18.50	AZ 7272

1 ....

'At 12.25.'

2 ....

'An hour.'

3 ....

'At ten to six.'

C Future perfect or future continuous?

You may not agree with these predictions but you can choose the right verb form anyway!

1 By 2025 the first humans .... (land) on the planet Mars.

2 In the next hundred years, the Netherlands .... (disappear) under water.

3 In the second decade of the 21st century, people .... (eat) more genetically modified food.

4 By 2030 Chinese .... (become) the language of international scientific communication.

5 Many people .... (live) to over 100 as medical science advances.

FUTURE (3)

USES

8 Future events still in progress

If an event is still in progress at a future time, we use the continuous form:

This time next year I**'ll be lying** on a beach in the Bahamas.

During the seminar you**'ll be learning** about negotiation strategies.

The future continuous is also used to talk about arrangements:

During your visit you**'ll be staying** at the Plaza hotel and **meeting** the commercial attaché. You**'ll** also **be visiting** some of the most important potential clients.

9 Making polite enquiries

The future continuous can be used to ask a question without giving the impression that we want to influence or direct people's actions. Compare:

Will you **be staying** for dinner? (an enquiry about plans)

Will you **stay** for dinner? (an invitation)

10 Using the present simple after *if*, *when*, *until*, *as soon as*

In time clauses we use the present simple to refer to the future. It is incorrect to use *will* in a time clause:

If you **give** us a discount, we'll place a bulk order.

Switch off the lights *when* you **leave**.

We won't begin *until* everyone **arrives**.

I'll give you a ring *as soon as* I **get** there.

11 Stating conditions

If a condition has to be met before something else can happen, we use the present perfect to refer to the future event in the time clause beginning with *if*, *when*, *until*, *as soon as*:

I can't go *if* I **haven't obtained** a visa.

I'll send you an e-mail *when* I**'ve made** all the arrangements.

We won't make a decision *until* we **have consulted** everyone.

I'll get back to you *as soon as* I**'ve spoken** to my boss.

12 Announcing official plans and arrangements

The infinitive is used to make official announcements:

Lear Corporation is **to axe** 2,800 jobs.

The president is **to visit** Iran next month.

The verb *to be* is often omitted in newspaper headlines:

BERLIN TO SPEED CUT IN CORPORATE TAXES

CENTRAL AMERICA TO GET $6bn AID

PRACTICE

A Travel arrangements

A group of travel agents has been invited by a tour operator on a familiarisation trip so that they can find out more about the holidays they sell. Look at the itinerary and complete the tour description below with the future continuous form of the words in brackets.

North India Tour

Day 1 BA flight London Gatwick → New Delhi; check-in at Whispering Palms Hotel

Day 2 Exploration of ancient walled city of Old Delhi; visit to Jama Masjid, the largest mosque in India

Day 3 Travel by coach to the deserted red sandstone city of Fatehpur Sikri

Day 4 Shopping in Agra; Taj Mahal visit at sunset

Day 5 Return journey to New Delhi and return flight via Goa

On the first day you'll be flying British Airways to New Delhi. On arrival there'll be a short tour of the city with its wide boulevards and impressive government buildings. We ....[1] (stay) at the Whispering Palms, which is a pleasant four-star hotel. The next day we ....[2] (explore) the city of Old Delhi and ....[3] (visit) Jama Masjid, the biggest mosque in India. Then on the third day we ....[4] (take) a coach to Fatehpur Sikri, built by the Emperor Akbar as his capital. We check into a hotel and the next day, after some shopping in the bazaar, we ....[5] (visit) the Taj Mahal at sunset, the best time to see it in its full splendour. On the Friday we ....[6] (return) to Delhi for a flight to Goa Airport and we ....[7] (transfer) to another hotel for a rest before flying back to London.

B *if, when, until, as soon as*

Complete these sentences with an appropriate form of the verbs in brackets. (There may be more than one possible answer.)

1 I .... (get) in touch when I .... (return) from the Middle East.

2 If they .... (shut down) the plant, a lot of people .... (lose) their jobs.

3 We .... (start) until everyone .... (be) here.

4 He can't make a decision until he .... (see) the president.

5 A project to create a bacterial cell from inanimate chemicals .... (go ahead) as soon as it .... (receive) approval from an ethics committee.

C Announcements

Write suitable headlines for the first lines of these articles.

1 Shoppers in the EU will be getting a core set of consumer rights under new legislation which Brussels will reveal this week.

2 China and the European Union put aside their differences on Friday, agreeing to hold a summit soon and to cooperate more closely.

UNIT 5

Conditionals

CONDITIONALS (1)

USES *If* introduces a *condition* – something may or may not happen depending on the circumstances. Conditional sentences have a number of uses.

1 Stating a general rule

If can be used to say what generally happens when something else happens. Both verbs in this type of sentence are in the present simple tense:

If you **order** in bulk, you usually **get** a discount.

If the paperwork **is** incomplete, the goods **are** often held up.

2 Speculating about the future

If can also be used to speculate about the future consequences of a specific event. In this case, the verb in the second part of the sentence is preceded by *will*.

If I **do** an MBA, I**'ll improve** my job prospects.

If we **break into** the Indian market, our turnover **will increase** substantially.

If our main competitor **goes** bankrupt, we**'ll increase** our market share.

The use of the present tense in the first part of the sentence indicates that the situation is *possible:* doing an MBA is feasible, breaking into the Indian market is seen as quite likely, the competitor may well go bankrupt.

Note that it is incorrect to use *will* with the first verb:

NOT *If I will do an MBA ...

3 *if* and *unless*

Unless often replaces *if* ... + negative expression:

If you don't wear a suit and tie, you won't be allowed into the club.

You won't be allowed into the club **unless** you wear a suit and tie.

We'll stop the meeting now **if** there is nothing else to discuss.

We'll stop the meeting now **unless** there is something else to discuss.

4 Promising and threatening

Conditional statements can function as either promises, warnings or threats. (But note that *unless* cannot be used to make a promise.)

If you order now, you**'ll** get a free gift. (promise)

We **won't** be able to do business with you **unless** you comply with our ethical policy. (warning)

Unless we receive payment by the end of the week, we **will** be forced to consider legal action. (threat)

PRACTICE

A It's generally the case

Match the sentence halves.

1 If the government lowers interest rates,
2 If you want to play golf well,
3 If inflation is high,
4 If the national currency is strong,
5 If you have an offshore bank account,
6 If you pay people peanuts,
7 If a firm doesn't advertise,

a) it loses market share.
b) people tend not to save.
c) it is more difficult to export.
d) you get monkeys.
e) you have to practise regularly.
f) it makes borrowing easier.
g) you don't pay income tax.

B Future consequences

Write what you will or may do in these situations.

1 if your car is stolen
2 if a close colleague gets married
3 if you are offered a better-paid job abroad
4 if your firm is taken over by a competitor
5 if you have to give a presentation in English
6 if your computer is infected with a virus

C *if* / *unless*

Complete each sentence with *if* or *unless*.

1 .... you don't have persistence, you can't be a good salesperson.
2 We don't employ people .... they're flexible and keen to work hard.
3 .... you do business abroad, it's a good idea to learn about the local culture.
4 .... you encounter any problems with your mobile phone, we will provide a complete repair service.
5 .... you call to tell me you're not coming, I'll see you tomorrow afternoon.
6 Don't promise anything .... you're completely sure.
7 Your presentation will be better .... you make good eye contact with the audience.
8 .... you increase sales by over 20%, the company will pay you a performance bonus.

CONDITIONALS (2)

USES

5 Imagining

If + past simple is used to refer to less probable situations. *Would / should / could / might* precede the verb in the subordinate clause:

If every piece of mail **was** personalised with your company logo or message, your customers **might** be very impressed.

Imagine what **would** happen **if** all the world's stock exchanges **crashed**.

If we **hired** a factoring agency, we **could** recover our debts more easily.

It is possible to use *if I were* or *if I was* in both formal and informal styles but *if I were* is considered more correct.

If I **were** rich, I **would buy** a Ferrari.

6 Bargaining

It is common to make hypothetical statements in negotiations. Compare:

a) If you **give** us 5% discount, we**'ll** make a repeat order of 5,000 units. (This is almost a promise.)

b) If you **gave** us 5% discount, we**'d** make a repeat order of 5,000 units. (This is a more tentative offer.)

You may therefore want to use *if* + past verb + *would* as an opening move in a negotiation, in order to test the ground.

7 *Provided* (*that*) / *so long as* / *on condition* (*that*)

When stating a condition it is also possible to use *provided that*, *so long as* or *on condition that*. It is not necessary to say or write *that*:

Provided (**that**) they **don't go** back on their offer, we'll sign the agreement next week.

We'll be happy to work with you **so long as** you pay half of the advertising costs.

We might be able to reduce the number of hours worked **on condition (that)** there is an increase in productivity.

PRACTICE

A Imagining

Write what you think might happen in the following (unlikely) situations.

1 if the world was governed by a Communist superpower
2 if your husband or wife was offered a good position in Iceland
3 if you stood for the presidential elections
4 if the sale of alcohol was banned in Europe
5 if you were accused of selling your country's military secrets

B Bargaining

Complete the sentences with the correct form of the verbs in brackets as in the example.

1 If you ..give.. (give) me 90 days to pay, I'll buy.. (buy) right now.
2 If you .... (give) me a special price, I .... (put in) a bigger order.
3 I .... (take) last year's stock if you .... (take off) 15%.
4 I .... (purchase) the equipment if you .... (throw in) the accessories.
5 How long .... (you hold) your prices if we .... (order) today?
6 If I .... (pay) cash, how much discount .... (you allow)?

C Negotiating positions

Expand the prompts to make conditional sentences with a past verb as in the example.

1 firm orders in advance — reduce the price by 10%?
If I gave you firm orders in advance, would you reduce the price by 10%?
2 make a repeat order — agree to split the transport costs 50–50?
....
3 ensure free maintenance — buy a new photocopier from us?
....
4 buy the turbo-diesel model — install air conditioning and a GPS free of charge?
....

D *provided (that), so long as, on condition (that)*

Complete the sentences with *provided that*, *so long as* or *on condition that*.

1 I agree to work seven days a week ...
2 I agree to take a cut in salary ...
3 We agree to make a special delivery ...

CONDITIONALS (3)

USES

8 Speculating about the past

When talking about things which did not happen in the past (and the consequences if they had happened) we use *if* + past perfect together with *would / could / might* + *have* + past participle:

If the price-earnings ratio **had been** higher, I **would have bought** some shares.

If we **had anticipated** the crash, we **wouldn't have lost** so much money.

The merger **could have succeeded if** the management styles **hadn't been** so different.

The presentation **might have been** better **if** she **had felt** more confident.

Note that in American English *would have* is possible in both clauses:

I **would have told** you **if** I **would have known** earlier.

9 Mixed conditionals

Not all sentences containing *if* follow the same patterns as those presented on this page and on pages 34 and 36. The sequence of tenses depends on the meaning that has to be conveyed.

If Robert **wasn't** so lazy, he **could have been** promoted. (He is permanently lazy which explains why he failed to get promotion.)

If you **had set off** earlier, you **would be** there by now. (This is true at the moment of speaking; the second part of the sentence does not refer to the past so *would have been* is incorrect.)

If you **will come** this way, **I'll show** you to Mrs Harvey's office. (*Will* can be used after *if* in polite requests.)

I**'ll lend** you 1,000 euros **if** it**'ll help** you set up your business. (There is nothing conditional about this sentence; the advantage is the result of the gift of money. Here *if* means *if it is true that.*)

We **would** be grateful **if** you **would** send us your payment made out to the order of 'InfoMart'. (This is a polite request.)

The verbs in both parts of the sentence are in the present simple tense when giving a warning or instruction or when making an invitation.

If the red light **comes on**, then **turn off** the machine immediately.

If Mrs Olsen **calls**, **tell** her I'm in a meeting.

If you **need** it, **ask** for help.

PRACTICE

A A negotiation breakdown

Read the following story and write how you would have reacted if you had been in John Dee's or Mrs Han's position.

John Dee imports microwave ovens from Korea and has been working satisfactorily with the same supplier for five years. Recently he travelled to Korea to meet the supplier and negotiate a reimbursement for a shipment of appliances that John's customers had sent back because of a serious manufacturing defect.

He met the Korean company's representative Mrs Han, who insisted she could not compensate John financially but would replace the defective appliances. John refused this offer, saying that this gesture would not in itself be sufficient to restore his reputation with his customers.

John was booked on a plane leaving that afternoon and could see little point in continuing the discussion. He was getting more impatient with the apparent lack of progress and stood up angrily and walked out of the discussion. Mrs Han was embarrassed and did not wish to lose face by asking him to return to the room.

John Dee now buys his microwaves from Taiwan at a higher unit price.

B The credit crunch

Read the text and say what you would have done if you had been able to influence events.

In August 2007 problems with the repayment of subprime mortgages in the US meant that thousands of people lost their homes because they could no longer pay back the money they owed. In January 2008 the investment bank Bear Stearns collapsed, followed by Lehman Brothers in September. The British bank Northern Rock also ran into trouble and was nationalised in February 2008. In 2009 the US government provided $700bn for a bank bailout.

At the end of that year, it was reported that Wall Street employees had been given more than $18bn in bonuses.

C Mixed conditionals

Read the following sentences and answer the questions about each one.

1 If he hadn't bought a second home in the country, he wouldn't be so short of money now.
   a) Did he buy a second home? b) Is he short of money?

2 If he had bought a second home in the country, he would be short of money now.
   a) Did he buy a second home? b) Is he short of money?

3 If she weren't so busy, she would have given you a hand.
   a) Is she busy? b) Did she help?

4 If she had been busy, she wouldn't have given you a hand.
   a) Was she busy? b) Did she help?

UNIT 6 Verb combinations

VERB COMBINATIONS (1)

FORM Verbs are often followed by another verb:

I **enjoy reading**.

She **denies selling** secrets.

He **doesn't recall meeting** him.

You **deserve to get** promotion.

I **didn't choose to do** this job.

I **don't want to go**.

USES 1 Verb + verb + *-ing*

The *-ing* form focuses on:

a) an action or state before the action of the first verb:

She admitted **taking** a bribe.

He misses **seeing** his wife and children.

She finished **doing** her accounts yesterday.

b) the activity itself. The second verb functions like a noun:

I dislike **travelling**.

She recommends **selling** the shares now.

They have postponed **launching** the new model.

Some common verbs that are followed by *-ing* forms:

admit	appreciate	contemplate	give up	involve
deny	enjoy	consider	carry on	mean
look forward to	mind	justify	can't stand	remember
anticipate	resent	warrant	detest	recollect
risk	recommend	delay	miss	
jeopardise	suggest	put off	avoid	

Note that synonyms and antonyms follow the same pattern.

PRACTICE

A Verb + verb + *-ing*

Match the sentence halves.

1 I'm looking forward to
2 I don't remember
3 He's decided to give up
4 Borrowing any more money would involve
5 She loves the sound of her voice and carried on

a) signing anything like that.
b) talking for half an hour.
c) increasing our debt–equity ratio.
d) smoking cigars for health reasons.
e) seeing you in Milan soon.

B Sentence transformation

Use the words in brackets to complete the second sentence so that it has a similar meaning to the first one.

a) Travelling doesn't bother me as long as there are no delays. (mind)

I don't ....

b) In my job I have to meet many people. (involve)

My job ....

c) I certainly did not pass on any trade secrets. (deny)

I firmly ....

d) There's a danger we will lose business to our competitors. (risk)

We ....

e) Why don't you get in touch with the commercial attaché? (suggest)

She ....

f) We fully expect to double our turnover in the next two years. (anticipate)

We ....

g) He was late so I didn't see him. (miss)

He was late so ....

h) Why on earth did you spend so much on entertainment? (justify)

How can you ....

VERB COMBINATIONS (2)

USES

2 Verb + *to*-infinitive

The *to*-infinitive form focuses on:

a) a purpose:

She **wishes to ask** you a favour.

She **intends to complain**.

They**'ve decided to go ahead** with the idea.

This report **attempts to explain** why a change is necessary.

b) a future situation:

They are **planning to launch** a takeover bid.

I**'ve arranged to see** the financial people tomorrow.

I **expect to see** them in Taiwan shortly.

Estefan **is hoping to study** law at Harvard.

Some common verbs that are followed by *to*-infinitive forms:

intend	attempt	promise	plan	guarantee	claim
mean	try	undertake	arrange	offer	pretend
want	hope	forget	seem	fail	
wish	expect	remember	appear	neglect	

Note that synonyms and antonyms follow the same pattern.

3 Verb + object + *to*-infinitive

When we want to talk about two actions performed by different people, the verbs are separated by an object:

He **didn't want** *me* **to attend** the meeting. (NOT *He didn't want that I attend ...)

They **don't allow** *you* **to smoke** at work. (NOT *They don't allow that ...)

A laptop **enables** *people* **to work** on a plane. (NOT *A laptop enables to work ...)

Some common verbs used with an object and a *to*-infinitive clause:

advise allow ask cause challenge choose defy enable encourage expect forbid force help inspire instruct intend invite lead leave mean oblige order pay permit persuade prefer programme recruit remind teach tell train trust urge use warn

PRACTICE

A Verb + *to*-infinitive

Use the words in brackets to complete the second sentence so that it has a similar meaning to the first one.

1 I'll do all I can to help. (promise)
She's ....

2 Send them the samples they requested – don't forget, will you? (remember)
Please ....

3 We will provide a 24-hour-a-day hotline. (undertake)
We ....

4 I anticipate receiving an answer soon. (expect)
I ....

5 If you like, we can send a replacement. (offered)
They have ....

6 She should have told them of the potential problem. (neglected)
She ....

7 I'm not sure, but I think there is a bug in the program. (appears)
There ....

8 She says she has the necessary authority. (claims)
She ....

B Verb + object + *to*-infinitive

The words in these sentences are in the wrong order. Rewrite them in the correct order.

1 me she to in myself taught believe
....

2 dirty they me to their do work paid
....

3 he perform a certain programmed robot to number tasks the of
....

4 federation the the rates cut minister to interest urged employers'
....

5 the from expertise to enabled joint benefit our us partner's venture
....

VERB COMBINATIONS (3)

4 Verb + object + verb + *-ing*

a) Some verbs are used with an object and a second verb ending in *-ing*

Verbs used in this way include:

catch describe discover feel find hear imagine keep leave like listen to notice observe prevent (from) save see send set show watch

Her comment **set** me **thinking**.

Outsourcing would **save** your **spending** money on permanent staff.

The white knight **prevented** the company from **being** taken over.

b) Verbs of perception

Not all of the action is seen or heard	*All of the action is seen or heard*
I **saw** a man **stealing** some clothes from a store.	I **saw** a man **steal** some clothes from a store.
He **watched** the crowd **leaving** the stadium.	He **watched** the crowd **leave** the stadium.
I **heard** a door **banging** repeatedly.	I **heard** a door **bang** once and then nothing.

5 Verb + infinitive without *to*

A few verbs used in the second position do not take *to*. These are *let*, *make* and *have* (in the sense 'cause to happen'):

We **let** them have a 10% discount. (NOT *let them to have)

Don't **make** me laugh. (NOT *make me to laugh)

Could you **have** Mrs Smith bring in the coffee now? (NOT *have Mrs Smith to bring)

6 Verb + *it* + object clause

When the object of a verb is a clause, *to*-infinitive or *-ing* structure, we use *it* after the verb to introduce the clause:

I find **it** impossible to understand their culture.

The government regards **it** as unnecessary to harmonise taxation.

She feels **it** is necessary to send a copy to absolutely everyone.

He found **it** worthwhile visiting the overseas subsidiaries.

PRACTICE

A Verbs of perception

There was a break-in at the headquarters of a company and the security guard has made a statement to the police saying what he saw and heard.

Complete the statement with the correct form of these verbs.

be	go through	feel	beat	move	whisper	come	lie	creep up

I have worked as a security guard here for six years and there has never been any trouble. But on the night in question at about 3am I was looking at the closed circuit TV screens in my room and saw someone ....[1] about in one of the offices. So I took my torch and went to investigate. I decided not to take the lift because an intruder would hear it ....[2] so I walked upstairs as quietly as I could. I stopped on the second floor and listened to my heart ....[3]. I imagined myself ....[4] attacked and I couldn't prevent myself from ....[5] afraid. I imagined myself ....[6] in a pool of blood in the deserted building. Then I continued up to the third floor and walked down the corridor. I could hear two people ....[7] to each other. I walked on. Through an open door I observed two masked men ....[8] the contents of the CEO's desk. Then after about 30 seconds – but it seemed like an eternity – I heard someone ....[9] behind me. Then everything went blank.

B Verb patterns

Correct the errors in these sentences.

1. I find impossible to work with him.
2. They made us to work extremely hard in my previous job.
3. She never let me to take any decisions.
4. Could you have Mr Clarke to prepare some statistics?
5. She's finding difficult to get used to the climate.
6. I feel is necessary to delegate more of the work.

VERB COMBINATIONS (4)

7 Verb + *for* + *to*-infinitive

Some verbs are followed by the preposition *for* and its object, then an infinitive:

He **arranged for** his secretary *to drive* him to the airport.

I **waited for** him *to get back* in touch.

They **called for** the union *to reconsider* its strike action.

These verbs can be used in this way:

appeal apply arrange ask call opt pay
plead vote wait wish yearn

8 Verb + possessive + verb + *-ing*

It is possible to introduce a possessive pronoun or a genitive between the first and second verbs. Thus *Please forgive me for asking* can be reformulated more formally as *Please forgive my asking*. Other verbs that follow this pattern are:

That would **entail** our making a concession.

This will **save** our wasting time.

They have **suggested** his going to the symposium.

He**'s looking forward to** our coming.

'I don't **mind** your being killed, but I **object to** your being taken prisoner.' (Lord Kitchener to the Prince of Wales, on his asking to fight during the First World War)

9 Special cases

Certain verbs are followed by either an infinitive or another verb + *-ing* but the choice leads to a change in the meaning:

I will never **forget** meeting Princess Diana. (= I will always remember)

I sometimes **forget** to wear my badge. (= fail to remember)

I **mean** to see her later this week. (= I intend to)

I could get a better job but it would **mean** moving. (= involve)

He was an alcoholic but **stopped** drinking. (= ceased)

He **stopped** to have a drink on the way back home. (= in order to)

She **remembered** to turn off her headlights. (= she didn't forget)

She **remembers** turning off her headlights. (= she has a clear memory of this)

Why don't you **try** giving the staff greater autonomy? (= experiment and see what happens)

He **tried** to learn car maintenance but gave up. (= attempted / made the effort)

PRACTICE

A Verb + *for* + *to*-infinitive

Match the sentence halves to make logical sentences.

1 The opposition party has called for
2 The conference organiser has arranged for
3 The production manager has been waiting for
4 The shareholders voted for
5 Her father paid for

a) the company to increase its share capital.
b) the spare parts to arrive.
c) the prime minister to resign.
d) her to go to an American university.
e) the delegates to stay in a four-star hotel.

B Special cases

Complete the extracts with the correct form of the verbs in brackets.

FT

1 The German Chancellor intervened yesterday in a dispute with the energy industry over plans to stop .... (use) nuclear power.

2 Apparently, the commissioner meant .... (inform) the investigators of the secret payments into a special fund but was persuaded not to do so.

3 I remember .... (go) to a private dinner with Princess Diana just a month before she died. When we walked out, the photographers' flash bulbs were so bright that it could have been midday.

4 Embarrassment yesterday as the wife of the prime minister attended the presentation of a football trophy. Unfortunately, someone forgot .... (tell) the photographers and the event had to be reprogrammed.

5 It could be that there is no crisis of faith in managers. It may simply be that suddenly everyone wants to be a management consultant or, failing that, an investment banker. If all those MBAs really do mean .... (work) for McKinsey&Company, The Boston Consulting Group, Goldman Sachs and all the rest, good luck to them. But if they believe that being a consultant or investment banker will mean .... (have) a balanced life with plenty of time for family and friends, they may be in for a rude shock.

UNIT 7

Passives

PASSIVES (1)

FORM We form the passive by using the appropriate tense of *to be* + a past participle:

Uranium **is mined** in Australia.

The company **was set up** in 1997.

A new extension **is being built**.

The company **has been taken over**.

It is also possible to use the passive with a modal verb:

The goods **will** be sent by rail.

The shipment **may** be delayed.

Tenders **should** be submitted in triplicate.

Helmets **must** be worn.

The subject of a passive verb corresponds to the object of an active verb:

	Subject		***Object***
Active	Mexicans	speak	Spanish
Passive	Spanish	is spoken	in Mexico.

Subject		***Object***
Richard Branson	founded	Virgin Records.
Virgin Records	was founded by	Richard Branson.

USES

1 Focusing on the action

We use a passive construction when we are not interested in who performs an action or it is not necessary to know:

The date **was changed**.

The missing file **has been found**.

He **has been promoted** to the post of sales director.

If we also want to mention who performs the action, we can use a phrase beginning with *by*:

The decision **was taken** *by the committee*.

The missing file **has been found** *by one of the cleaners*.

2 Focusing on information

In a passive sentence, the grammatical subject receives the focus:

The visiting delegation **was met** by the president at the airport.

Here the visiting delegation, rather than the president, is the centre of interest.

PRACTICE

A Passive verb forms

Match the sentence halves.

1 Your enquiry
2 Make sure that your mobile phone
3 All tenders and supporting documents
4 Your hotel booking
5 As requested, the sum of $75,000
6 The full conference programme

a) has been confirmed.
b) has been credited to your account.
c) has not yet been printed.
d) is switched off during important meetings.
e) must be returned by 31 March.
f) is being dealt with.

B Focusing on the action

Make these sentences passive. Use *by* only if it is necessary to say who did the action.

1 Karl Marx wrote *Das Kapital*.
2 They are repairing your car now.
3 Steve Jobs founded Apple Computers.
4 The board will discuss the proposal.
5 Did anyone inform Mrs Wilson?
6 They make Renault cars in Slovenia.
7 They have transferred him to the New York office.
8 The princess opened the new conference centre.
9 They had made a full investigation.
10 I didn't realise someone was listening to my telephone conversations.

C Focusing on information

Read the text and rewrite the information, changing the focus as in the example.

DEALING WITH MESSAGES

Written documents and messages land on your desk all the time and you need to process them efficiently. Here are a few tips.

- You should read through documents quickly and absorb their main information content.
- If you need to file a written document, you can write the file name on the document.
- If a written message requires action, you should make a note, for example on a Post-it™.
- You should dispose of all messages once you have dealt with them.

Dealing with messages

Written documents and messages land on your desk all the time and ....need to be processed........ efficiently. Here are a few tips.

- Documents ....[1] quickly and their main information content ....[2].
- If ....[3], the file name ....[4].
- If a written message requires action, ...[5], for example on a Post-it™.
- ....[6].

PASSIVES (2)

USES

3 Describing a process or procedure

We use the passive because we are more concerned with the process itself than with who carries it out. For example, here is a description of the wine-making process:

Wine **is made** from the fermented juice of grapes. Grapes **are picked** at optimum sugar / acidity levels. After picking, the grapes **are taken** to the winery, **de-stemmed** and **crushed** in a variety of presses. The juice **is** then **clarified** by settling or by centrifuge, yeast and sugar **are added** and the wine **is left** to ferment in tanks. When fermentation **is finished**, the wine **is poured** into a clean tank to stabilise. It **can** then **be filtered** and **bottled** and left to mature.

4 Writing in a formal style

When writing in a formal style (e.g. reports, minutes of meetings) we often choose an impersonal style by using the passive and beginning sentences with *it*:

It was agreed to increase the share capital.

It was considered to be an unacceptable alternative.

It has now **been decided** to postpone the proposed construction.

Another common way of reporting what is said or thought is to use *it* + passive + *that*-clause:

It was agreed that the share capital should be increased.

It was felt that some economies had to be made.

Other verbs used in this pattern include:

announce claim discover estimate expect know mention
propose recommend suggest think understand

5 Reporting unconfirmed information

When the statement is speculative, we use the passive of *say*, *think*, *consider* or *believe* followed by an infinitive. This structure is common in newspaper reporting:

The minister **is said to be** in favour of decreasing corporation tax.

The board **is thought to be** in favour of a merger.

The terrorists **are believed to want** a new ceasefire.

PRACTICE

A Check your understanding

Are these sentences true or false?

1 Passives are used when we are interested in who has done something rather than what is done.
2 Passives are used when the focus is on what is done rather than the people who perform the action.
3 The object of an active verb corresponds to the subject of a passive verb.
4 Passives are common in an informal style.
5 The passive is often used to describe the stages of a process.

B Active or passive?

Complete this advertisement with either the active or the passive as appropriate.

Communicado's presentation skills training courses .... [1] (tailor) to each client's individual needs, so the main focus is on the type of presentations that .... [2] (give) by the participants in their everyday working lives. Courses .... [3] (conduct) either on a one-to-one basis or in groups. They are highly participative and .... [4] (design) to be enjoyable as well as instructive.

Communicado .... [5] (encourage) clients to .... [6] (build) on their existing social communication skills. Through a number of interesting techniques we .... [7] (show) clients how time can .... [8] (save) in preparation, how body language can .... [9] (use) to maximum effect and how visual aids can .... [10] (create) for maximum impact.

For more details on how Communicado can .... [11] (help) your company improve its business presentations, call 0800 222 4567 now.

C Describing a process

The following passage describes the production of paper. Complete the passage with the correct form of the verbs in brackets, using the passive when necessary.

From trees to pulp

The trees .... [1] (transport) to the paper mill by lorry, train or ship. First, the bark .... [2] (remove). This .... [3] (burn) at a later stage so that energy can .... [4] (generate) for the paper-making process. Then the logs .... [5] (cut) into chips and .... [6] (cook) under high pressure for four hours to make paper pulp. Next the pulp .... [7] (bleach) to .... [8] (remove) dirt spots and .... [9] (improve) its ageing properties.

From pulp to paper

The manufacturing process also .... [10] (require) chemicals to strengthen the paper. The fibres .... [11] (mix) with additives and .... [12] (dilute) with water. This mixture .... [13] (spray) onto the paper machine where it .... [14] (press), then .... [15] (dry) and .... [16] (wind) onto one large reel which .... [17] (weigh) up to 20 tons. Each part of the process .... [18] (control) by computers, which automatically .... [19] (correct) any errors.

UNIT 8

Modal verbs (expressing subjective viewpoints)

ABILITY

FORM A modal always comes before another verb:

You **must go**.

A modal is not followed by *to*:

NOT *You must to go.

The form of a modal never changes; there is no *s* on the third person, no *-ing* form, no past tense:

NOT *You musts go, *musting, *You musted.

Questions are formed by inverting the modal and the subject:

Must you go?

Modals are not used together:

NOT *She will must go.

USES Modal verbs are auxiliary verbs that express the speaker's judgement about the likelihood or desirability of a situation. All modals can be used to talk about probability or possibility; modals can also be used to express interpersonal meanings such as obligation or willingness.

Ability

1 Saying that someone knows how to

We use *can* to say that someone is able / not able to do something:

Our new divisional manager **can** speak four languages fluently.

He **can't** drive; he's never learnt how to.

We also use *can* to say that machines are able to perform certain tasks:

The new photocopier **can** print out a whole book in less than five minutes.

2 Talking of a past ability

He **could** play the piano when he was five years old.

This sentence refers to an ability that was not limited to just one occasion. If we want to speak of one event we use *managed to* or *was able to*:

After six hours of negotiation, we finally **managed to** make some progress. (NOT *we could)

After six hours of negotiation, we **were** finally **able to** make some progress.

The negative form is, however, possible for just one occasion:

We **couldn't** get tickets for the opera – they were all sold out.

3 Indicating disapproval when something is or was not done

She **could** make more of an effort. (= she is able to, but doesn't)

You **could have told** me beforehand – I needed to know. (= you were able to, but didn't)

PRACTICE

A Abilities

Match the personal qualities 1–7 with the abilities a–g.

If you	*you can*
1 are computer literate,	a) work well on your own.
2 are trilingual,	b) use different types of software.
3 are good at mental arithmetic,	c) solve problems rationally.
4 are autonomous,	d) be a good leader.
5 have a creative personality,	e) calculate quickly in your head.
6 have a logical mind,	f) speak three languages.
7 are decisive and people accept your authority,	g) bring new ideas to projects.

B Past abilities

Complete the sentences with *could* or *managed to*.

1 After a lot of discussion we .... strike a deal.
2 He's so lazy – I really feel he .... try harder.
3 I thought I was going to miss the plane but I .... get to the airport on time.
4 When I was younger, I .... run several kilometres without feeling tired.
5 She .... find a good job despite her lack of formal qualifications.
6 When we lived near the beach, we .... go swimming every day.
7 She .... have left me a message – how was I supposed to know?

C Indicating disapproval

React to these situations with *could have*.

1 Why didn't she ring to tell me she would be late?
2 She had the facts and figures but left me in the dark.
3 It wasn't worth our taking a taxi – the station was within walking distance.
4 It took six days for the letter to arrive and we both have e-mail.

OBLIGATION, PROHIBITION

USES

1 Saying what is compulsory

We use *must* or *has / have to* to indicate what is compulsory in the present and future:

'Any change in taxation **must** be fair, fiscally responsible and **must** avoid simply shifting the burden from the rich to the middle class,' the president said.

All travellers to China **have to** be in possession of a visa.

Must can also be used in reported speech:

The Chamber of Commerce and Industry said the government **must** act to tackle traffic congestion.

If something was necessary or obligatory in the past, we use *had to,* and for the future we use *will have to*:

When we lived in Lisbon, we **had to** learn some Portuguese.

We **will have to** evaluate the new procedure regularly.

The absence of future obligation is expressed by *will not / won't have to*:

If you open a bank account with us, you **won't have to** pay interest if you go overdrawn.

2 Imposing an obligation on ourselves

We prefer to use *must* when we oblige ourselves to do something. We prefer *have to* when the obligation is imposed by other people or external circumstances:

I **must** remember to get in touch with Mr Gonzales. I keep forgetting.

I **must** buy my wife a present before I go home.

We **have to** wear a uniform at work – it's not our choice.

I enjoy going to conferences unless I **have to** make a presentation.

3 Freedom to choose

If you *do not have to* do something, there is no obligation – you are free to act:

I can work from home so I **don't have to** go into the office very often.

4 Saying that something is prohibited

We use *must not* (NOT *do not have to) to say that something is forbidden or very unacceptable:

Passengers **must not** smoke during the flight.

You **mustn't** enter a joint venture unless both parties benefit from the deal.

Cannot and *may not* are also used if something is forbidden because of a rule or a law:

Retailers **cannot** / **may not** sell below cost price in some countries.

PRACTICE

A Rules and regulations

Complete the sentences so that they are true for your country. Use *have to*, *don't have to* and *must not*.

1. You .... carry a gun.
2. You .... pay to use buses and trams.
3. You .... vote if you are over 18.
4. You .... drink alcohol at work.
5. You .... pay to drive on a motorway.
6. You .... declare income earned abroad.
7. You .... wear a seat belt when driving a car.

B Rules at work

Complete the sentences so that they are true for your job situation. Use *have to*, *don't have to* and *must not*.

1. You .... take home company equipment.
2. You .... wear a badge.
3. You .... wear a tie if you are a man.
4. You .... wear jeans at work.
5. You .... clock in when you arrive.
6. You .... wear a dress or a suit if you are a woman.

C Signs and notices

What can you say about these signs using *have to*, *don't have to*, *must* and *must not*?

POSSIBILITY

USES

1 Expressing possibility

We use *can* to say that something is possible and *cannot* or *could not* if something is impossible:

Mathematics **can** be really interesting.

In some cases, customs clearance **can** be difficult to obtain.

You **can't** fly to Dover – there isn't an airport.

Protectionism **can't** be the final answer to a country's economic problems.

I **couldn't** tell you exactly what our turnover is but it's over £100m.

If a situation is possible but it is not certain that it will happen or be possible, we use *could*:

A lot of accidents at work **could** be avoided.

If we outsourced more, we **could** save a lot of money.

2 Saying something was possible in the past

We use either *could* or *used to be able to*:

Twenty years ago you **could** walk in the fields but they've all been built on now.

You **used to be able to** put coins in telephone boxes but not now.

We use *could not* or *couldn't* if something was impossible:

Twenty years ago you **couldn't** buy a computer as cheaply as you can now.

This can be reformulated as:

Twenty years ago you **didn't use to be able to** buy a computer as cheaply as you can now.

3 Talking about past opportunities

A past opportunity which was not fulfilled is expressed using *could have* and a past participle:

She **could have gone** to Harvard but she went to Yale instead.

He could have been a member of parliament but he preferred to stay out of politics.

PRACTICE

A *can*

Make sentences from this table with *can*.

Learning a foreign language Entertaining overseas customers Being in charge of a new project Setting up in business Negotiating a contract	can	occasionally sometimes often	be	hard work. good fun. challenging. a waste of time. painful. boring.

B *could / couldn't*

Rewrite the sentences with *could* or *couldn't*.

1 If we diversified, we would be able to offer a wider range of products.
2 If I had stayed in the States, I would have been able to get a better job.
3 In the 1990s it was possible to make a fortune as a 'golden boy'.
4 She had an opportunity to do an MBA but decided it was too much work.
5 Forty years ago you used to be able to buy cigarettes in packets of five.
6 Before privatisation it wasn't possible to buy shares in British Telecom.

C Missed opportunities

Read the story and list four missed opportunities using *could have*.

As a young man Peter Metro was a gifted musician who once had a record in the top 20. But he decided to abandon music and study ocean engineering at Florida Atlantic University instead. After four years there he graduated and was offered a research post in the faculty but by that time he had decided he wanted to see the world and spent a year travelling Europe. In Italy he happened to meet the film director Roberto Bellini, who offered him a role in his latest film, but he turned it down because he had just accepted a job with a small firm specialising in the construction of racing catamarans. One day the famous skipper Chris Dickson asked him to sail with him during the Admiral's Cup but Peter decided not to because ...

LIKELIHOOD

USES A number of modal verbs are used to express degrees of certainty, according to the speaker's perception of the situation.

1 100% certain

The 21st century **will** be very different from the preceding 1,000 years. (an obvious prediction)

Economics **will** never be a precise science. (a general truth)

2 Very certain (based on deduction)

You **must** be very tired after such a long flight.

That **can't** be Rowena's car – she's driving to London today.

3 Probably

You **may well** have a point there.

Interest rates **could well** go up by a whole percentage point.

We **should** arrive before lunch if there's not too much traffic.

4 Likely (based on speculation)

Proposals to safeguard failing banks **could** undermine confidence in the City and raise the cost of capital to British banks. The Asssociation of British Insurers fears that the proposals as they stand **could** leave existing shareholders and investors facing serious losses.

The firm **may** be forced to make a number of employees redundant in the coming months but the situation **may** improve in the longer term.

Might suggests less certainty:

The president **might** survive the scandal but his chances look pretty slim.

5 Highly unlikely / impossible

You **won't** know Agnes – she's our new marketing person.

We **can't** meet such a short deadline.

PRACTICE

A Degrees of likelihood

This passage deals with the likelihood of an earthquake in the San Francisco Bay Area. Complete the passage with phrases a–h.

The next big earthquake in the Bay Area may come sooner than you think. There is a 67 percent chance of at least one earthquake of magnitude 7 or larger in the San Francisco Bay Area between 2010 and 2040. Such an earthquake ....[1].

Some scientists believe that the 67 percent probability estimate ....[2]. They have noted several instances of pairs of earthquakes of magnitude 6.5 or larger in northern California, and they are concerned that the Loma Prieta earthquake ....[3]. Other fault segments in northern California ....[4]. Therefore it seems prudent to consider the 67 percent chance of a large earthquake within the next 30 years as a minimum estimate.

Future studies are also likely to produce additional data that ....[5]. However, the major conclusions are not likely to change. Scientists agree that

- earthquakes of magnitude 7 and larger are highly likely within the Bay Area during the next few decades.
- each of these events ....[6] because each will probably be located closer to densely populated areas.
- action is needed now to reduce the damage and the number of deaths that ....[7] even if this ....[8].

From *United States Geological Survey*

a) might also be capable of producing large earthquakes
b) may be too low
c) could cause more damage than the Loma Prieta quake
d) will result in changes in probability estimates
e) could strike at any time, including today
f) could be the first quake of such a pair
g) may involve significant expense
h) could result from future major earthquakes

B Expressions of likelihood

What other expressions of likelihood are there in this passage?

PERMISSION, SUGGESTIONS, OFFERS

USES

1 Asking for and giving permission

Can is used to ask for and give permission:

'**Can** I use your mobile phone?' 'Sure, you **can** – go ahead.' / 'No, you **can't**.'

May and *could* are also used to ask for permission, but not to refuse permission. They are more formal than *can*:

'**May** I use your password?' 'No, I'm afraid you can't.' (NOT *I'm afraid you may not.)

'**Could** I come back later?' 'No, I don't think that'll be possible.' (NOT *No, you couldn't.)

If we want to talk about permission for a future action, we use the verbs *allow* or *permit*:

They won't **allow** / **permit** you to travel alone. (NOT *They won't can ...)

2 Making suggestions

I think you **should** upgrade your computer.

You **might** want to look at the new Compaq model.

Or you **could** add extra memory to your existing machine.

Shall I look at what it would cost?

3 Offering

Can we give you a lift into town?

Would you like me to give you a hand?

Shall I give you a hand? (Note that this is an offer in the present, not for the future.)

I'**ll** give you a hand if you like. (Note that the offer is made by *'ll,* not *will* or *shall.*)

Let me know if you need any help.

If you want to make an offer in a persuasive way, you can use *must*. (Note that there is no obligation here!)

You **must** come and visit me sometime.

➡ *Suggesting* page 140

PRACTICE

A Permission, suggestions or offers?

Are the following requests for permission (R), suggestions (S) or offers (O)? Write the appropriate letter in the space provided.

1 Shall we go for lunch? ....
2 May I sit here? ....
3 Shall I give you a lift into town? ....
4 Can I borrow the car this weekend? ....
5 Could I use your mobile phone? ....
6 You might like to check the exchange rate first. ....
7 Would you like us to send you a catalogue? ....
8 In my opinion you should sell your shares now. ....
9 Are you hot? I'll switch on the air conditioning if you like. ....

B Offers and suggestions

Complete the dialogue with these expressions.

Do you need any help	I'll give you	Shall I hold the door open
Would you like me	We must get together	

A It's been wonderful seeing you. ....[1] some time.
B Yes, that'd be very nice.
A ....[2] with your baggage?
B No, thanks. I can manage.
A Are you sure? ....[3] for you?
B Yes, please.
A ....[4] to call a taxi?
B No, thanks. I'll walk. It's not far.
A No, you can't possibly. Your cases are heavy. ....[5] a lift. It won't take me two minutes to get the car.
B Well, thank you very much. It's really very kind of you.
A Not at all. It's my pleasure.

WILLINGNESS, REFUSAL, PROMISES, THREATS, TYPICAL BEHAVIOUR

USES

1 Asking people if they don't mind

We use *will* or *would* to make a polite request or to ask someone if they are willing to assist:

Will you come this way?

Will you sign here, please?

Would you do me a favour?

Would you tell him that Mr Harvey phoned?

But a request can also function as a command:

Will you be here at 9 o'clock sharp, please?

2 Insisting

Will can mean 'to insist on doing something' even if it is inadvisable:

If you **will** smoke two packets a day, it's not surprising you've got a persistent cough.

3 Refusing

If you want to say that you are unwilling to do something, you can use *will not* or *won't*:

I **will not** tolerate her behaviour any longer.

Other people or things can also show unwillingness:

The car **won't** start. She **won't** ever do what I tell her to do.

4 Promising

If you make a firm commitment to do something in the future, you use *will*:

We **will** do everything in our power to satisfy your needs.

However, the promise may have a negative impact and is therefore interpreted as a threat:

Unless you comply, we **will** be forced to initiate legal proceedings.

5 Routine behaviour or general truths

Most days **I'll** get home at about 7.30pm but quite often later.

Murphy's Law states that if something can go wrong, it **will** go wrong.

Would is used to talk about actions that frequently happened in the past:

Our previous chairperson **would** always begin the annual general meeting with a joke.

PRACTICE

A Uses of *will* and *would*

Which of the following uses of *will* indicate refusal (R), a promise (P), a threat (T) or typical behaviour (TB)? Write the appropriate letter in the space provided.

1 I'll make sure John is informed. ....
2 Oil will float on water. ....
3 She won't listen. She's so stubborn. ....
4 Patrick will keep on asking stupid questions. ....
5 I'll take your calls for you while you're out. ....
6 Either I get the job or I'll leave the company. ....
7 I'll call him back when I've got a moment. ....
8 I've changed the battery but my mobile phone still won't work. ....
9 She will always be the first person to arrive on a Monday morning. ....
10 If you don't sign the new contract, we'll have to move you to another post. ....

B *will*, *won't* or *would*?

Rewrite the sentences with *will*, *won't* or *would*.

1 Accidents inevitably happen.
2 I promise to do my best.
3 She refuses to accept his authority.
4 If you don't pay, legal action is certain to be taken.
5 A fanatic is someone who can't change his mind and refuses to change the subject. (Winston Churchill)
6 If you insist on being rude, how can you expect people to like you?
7 He used to smoke a large cigar before making an important decision.
8 The product with the better-known brand name inevitably sells better than the other.

UNIT 9

Multi-word verbs

TYPES OF MULTI-WORD VERBS

Multi-word verbs are very frequent in English. There are over 3,000 of them with over 5,000 meanings! They are created when a verb, often a very common one such as *come*, *get*, *give*, *go*, *make*, *put*, *run*, *take* or *turn*, combines with 'particles' like *at, away*, *down*, *in*, *on*, *off*, *up* and so on.

Types of multi-word verbs

1 Without an object

The truck **broke down** on the freeway.

I'll be **tied up** all day so I can't see her until tomorrow.

I felt sick as the plane **took off**.

Her new book has just **come out**.

2 With an object – separable

Adverb particles can go before or after noun objects:

We've **brought forward** the meeting.

We've **brought** the meeting **forward**.

Could you **switch off** the computer?

Could you **switch** the computer **off**?

However, the particle cannot be used before a pronoun:

We've **brought** it **forward**. (NOT *We've brought forward it.)

Note that if the noun phrase is long, it is very unusual to separate the verb and particle. The second sentence below is unacceptable.

We've **narrowed** the number of choices **down** to three.

NOT *We've narrowed the number of choices down that we think are feasible to three.

3 With an object – inseparable

Some verbs are followed by a preposition. In this case, the preposition goes before the object:

We'll have to **look into** the matter. (NOT *look the matter into)

I'm **counting on** your support. (NOT *counting your support on)

4 With two particles

She is trying to **back out of** our agreement.

The austerity measures **came in for** a lot of criticism.

We're not prepared to **put up with** her absenteeism any longer.

PRACTICE

A With or without an object?

Complete the sentences which need an object with an appropriate object a–e.

1 Neither of the opponents would give in
2 Our policy is never to turn away
3 She's thought up
4 A number of reasons can account for
5 She came in for
6 I was completely taken in
7 I wonder when it will turn up
8 I don't understand what you're getting at
9 Crowds of people were turned away
10 Try to fix up

a) a lot of abuse.
b) a new name for the brand.
c) a customer.
d) a meeting with the director.
e) the change.

B Separable or inseparable?

Label the sentences acceptable (A) or unacceptable (U).

EXAMPLE:

We brought the meeting forward. ......A......
We brought forward the meeting. ......A......
We brought forward it. ......U......

1 We've sent off the catalogue to the printer's. ....
2 We've sent it off to the printer's. ....
3 We've sent off it to the printer's. ....

4 She wants to put off the meeting until next week. ....
5 She wants to put it off until next week. ....
6 She wants to put the meeting off until next week. ....

7 Could you go over the report again for me? ....
8 Could you go the report over for me? ....
9 Could you go it over for me? ....

10 We're trying to break into a new market. ....
11 We're trying to break a new market into. ....
12 We're trying to break it into. ....

13 We're going to phase out the old model. ....
14 We're going to phase the old model out. ....
15 We're going to phase it out. ....

UNDERSTANDING MULTI-WORD VERBS (1)

Many multi-word verbs are easy to understand:

Put the coin **in** the slot.

Could you **turn down** the volume?

In these examples the particle has an easily interpreted meaning. Others are not so easy:

A lot of executives **put in** over 50 hours a week. (= work)

She applied for the post but was **turned down**. (= refused)

It can help if you understand the meaning of the particle which combines with a verb.

1 *up*

a) increasing

We need to **build up** stocks in case there's a strike.

The economy is beginning to **pick up** again.

She's opened a new bank account and wants to **save up** for a new car.

b) advancing / coming closer

The New Media Marketing conference is **coming up** soon.

It's difficult to **keep up** with all the latest developments.

The car **drew up** beside us and the driver asked for directions.

c) inventing

The advertising agency is trying to **think up** a brilliant new slogan.

Where did you **dream up** that crazy idea?

He forgot his notes so he had to **make up** his speech as he went along.

d) completing

The final chapter **sums up** all the arguments.

There are a couple of points we need to **clear up**.

They've decided to **wind up** their operations in Ireland and relocate.

e) going wrong

Don't **mix up** the files or we'll never find the documents we need.

The office **slipped up** and the order was never sent.

The delay in the delivery of essential raw materials threatened to **hold up** production.

PRACTICE

A Multi-word verbs with *up*

Match the sentence halves.

1 He may break up
2 We need more facts to back up
3 Her name often comes up
4 I've been away so I need to catch up
5 If the bank refuses the loan,
6 The lawyer has drawn up

a) with what's been going on.
b) in conversation.
c) it'll mess up all our plans.
d) the terms of the contract.
e) under all the stress.
f) our arguments.

B Sentence completion

Complete the sentences with these verbs.

play up	follow up	pay up	work up	look up	face up to

1 He's too young to .... such a heavy responsibility.
2 The director will now .... the committee's suggestions.
3 I just can't .... any enthusiasm for the idea.
4 Now we have a new dynamic team, things will start to ....
5 Did the insurance company .... after all that argument?
6 The mechanism has begun to .... again and it needs an urgent repair.

C Sentence completion

Complete the sentences with these verbs. There are more verbs than necessary.

think up	turn up	save up	clear up	set up	keep up	hold up	take up	do up

1 How long did it take you to .... for a new yacht?
2 Can you help me .... this mess?
3 It's difficult to .... with all the new developments.
4 He gave his son some capital to .... his own business.
5 I don't want to .... you .... if you're in a hurry.
6 How did you .... such a clever way out of the difficulty?

UNDERSTANDING MULTI-WORD VERBS (2)

2 *down*

a) reducing

The economy is overheating and needs to **slow down**.

We've started to explore ways of **keeping down** costs.

The government intends to **water down** its commitment to a clean air policy.

b) coming to an end

The shipyard is due to **close down** at the end of the year.

Mr Holzer has **stepped down** as vice-president.

Talks **broke down** before a deal could be reached.

c) writing / recording

I've **put** your name **down** on the list.

Could you please **write down** your name and address.

Make sure you **note down** every word she says.

d) defeating

Eventually, he had to **back down** and apologise.

The army quickly **put down** the rebellion.

Another series of public sector strikes could **bring** the government **down**.

3 *over*

a) considering

Before I make any decision, I'll need to **talk** it **over** with my boss.

Give me a couple of days to **think** it **over**.

Do you have a few minutes to **look over** what I've written?

b) changes

Eurotunnel will **hand over** 40% of its after-tax profits to the UK and French governments from 2050 onwards.

There has recently been a hostile attempt to **take over** our company.

Swiss banks yesterday gained a significant victory in their attempt to **win over** US public opinion.

PRACTICE

A Multi-word verbs with *down*

Complete the sentences with these verbs.

play down	run down	break down	cut down	bring down	note down

1 The talks are likely to .... if both parties refuse a compromise.
2 The old system is being progressively .... and will soon be replaced.
3 Retailers are having to .... their prices to attract custom.
4 I'll just .... your address and phone number.
5 In a time of rising costs we should .... on our spending.
6 The minister is bound to .... the scale of the disaster.

B Multi-word verbs with *up*, *down* and *over*

Match the sentence halves.

1 We've kept our prices down but, as a result,
2 They're winding up their operations and
3 My father set up the company in 1982 and
4 The share price shot up 25%
5 The talks were on the point of breaking down
6 The prime minister stepped down when
7 Think it over and, if you agree to the terms,

a) I took over the business when he retired.
b) when we took over our nearest rival.
c) the factory will close down soon.
d) we'll draw up a contract.
e) we've had to cut down on production costs.
f) she failed to win over public opinion.
g) when the Swedish ambassador came up with a brilliant solution.

UNDERSTANDING MULTI-WORD VERBS (3)

4 *off*

a) beginning

After a slow start, sales are finally about to **take off**.

The finance minister's declaration **sparked off** a great deal of speculation.

The report **set off** a wave of early selling in the Treasury market.

b) stopping

The leader of the opposition said he was reluctant to **break off** talks with the government.

The crew of the damaged Mir space station were forced to **call off** a planned docking with a cargo ship after a computer failure.

They've decided to **put off** the meeting until next week.

c) reducing

Sales should **level off** now after reaching 375,000 units last year.

The novelty of frequent travel tends to **wear off** pretty quickly.

Interest rates have been raised to **cool off** inflationary pressures.

5 *on*

continuing

Don't bother about me; just **carry on** with what you're doing.

The law suit **dragged on** and on for eight years.

Could you **hold on** for a few moments while I consult with my colleague?

6 Verbs with two particles followed by an object

Examples include:

We need to **come up with** a solution soon. (= find / produce)

We should try to **cut down on** spending. (= reduce)

I'll **get on to** Mrs Butler and give you her reply shortly. (= contact)

It's difficult to **get on with** Mr Grundy; he's so bad-tempered. (= see eye to eye)

It's vital to **keep up with** developments in information technology. (= be fully informed)

I **look forward to** seeing you again. (= anticipate with pleasure)

We're late so we'll have to work hard to **make up for** lost time. (= compensate for)

The failure can be **put down to** poor quality control. (= explained by / attributed to)

She wants more responsibility and has **put in for** promotion. (= applied for)

I've had to **put up with** a lot of unfair criticism. (= tolerate)

PRACTICE

A Particles and their meaning

1 Match each particle 1–5 with one of the meanings a–e.

1 up	a) writing/recording
2 down	b) considering
3 on	c) beginning
4 off	d) continuing
5 over	e) completing

2 Combine the verbs below with a particle above to make a multi-word verb and then indicate its area of meaning.

1 think ....over = considering........
2 spark ....
3 wind ....
4 sum ....
5 look ....
6 note ....
7 keep ....
8 back ....

B Sentence rearrangement

The words in these sentences are in the wrong order. Rewrite them in the correct order.

1 need we to for lost time make up
2 the up firm strong against ran competition
3 a of have people put chairperson's for the number job in
4 back want to agreement out they of the
5 round after a drafting a to delay he long got reply
6 thinks Roger he's an up with come problems answer our to

C A phone conversation

Complete the phone conversation with these verbs and particles.

call	fix	get	read	hold	put	tied	back (x3)	on	through	up (x2)

A Multiplex plc, can I help you?

B Yes, I'd like to speak to Mr Webster, please.

A Certainly, I'll just .... you ....[1]. Sorry, the line's busy. Would you like to ....[2] or ....[3] later?

B Um, could you take a message?

A Certainly.

B Could you tell him that I'll be ....[4] all day Friday. So if he can ....[5] to me we can ....[6] another time to meet.

A Right, and your name?

B It's Kamal Ahmed on 0207 542 6688.

A I'll just .... that ....[7] to you. Kamal Ahmed on 0207 542 6688.

B Great. Thanks for your help.

UNIT 10 Adverbs

ADVERB POSITION AND USES (1)

FORM

He **rarely** drinks alcohol.

I can **usually** take at least an hour for lunch.

She has **always** been devoted to the company.

She speaks Spanish **very well**.

From these examples we see that the adverb goes:

a) before the main verb
b) between a modal (e.g. *could, will*) and the main verb
c) between two auxiliaries for frequency adverbs
d) after the direct object (NOT *She speaks very well Spanish.).

The adverb comes after the verb *to be*:

I am **still** waiting.

She was **obviously** delighted.

We are **always** ready to pay you a visit.

USES

1 Saying how, where, when or how often something happens or is done

	quickly / by train / alone.
He went	there / home / up to the second floor.
	recently / a couple of weeks ago.

2 Modifying verbs and adjectives

Prices have gone up **excessively**.

Microchips are **very** cheap.

She **almost** forgot to take her passport.

She is **terribly** forgetful.

His idea is **completely** out of the question.

She is **absolutely** fabulous.

They **totally** disagree with our position.

It's been **remarkably** successful.

3 Describing the rate of change

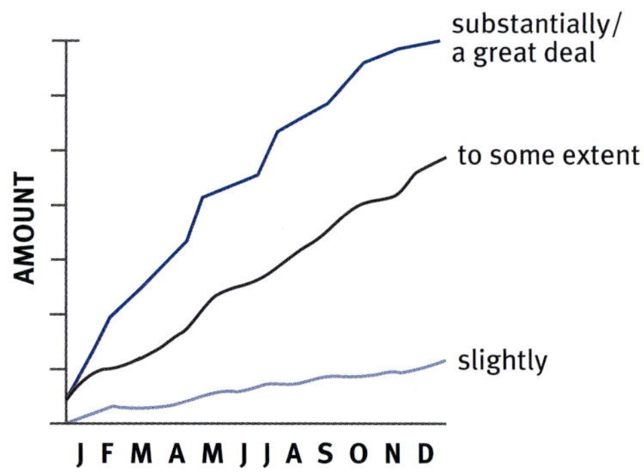

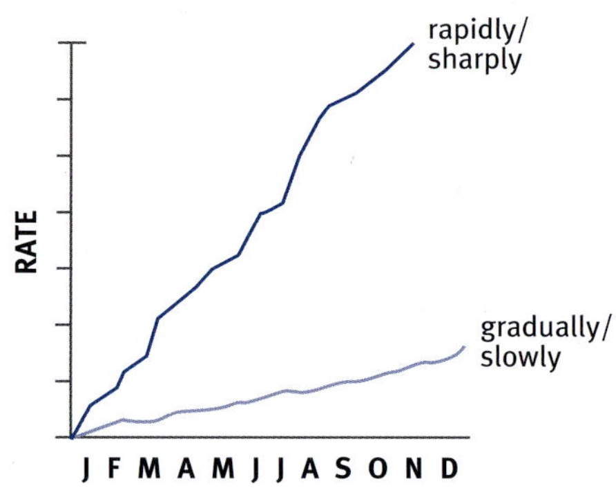

PRACTICE

A Sentence rearrangement

The words in these sentences are in the wrong order. Rewrite them in the correct order.

1 for confirmation I still am waiting
2 I wear never jeans at work
3 he speaks very well Greek
4 cheaper I will be probably able to get it
5 to welcome visitors I always am pleased
6 her idea completely is absurd

B Adverb position

Complete the e-mail by placing the adverbs in the correct position on each line.

very Hi! Thanks for your last mail. I'm ^ sorry I haven't	very
got back to you sooner but we've been rushed	terribly
in the office. We seem to be extremely busy.	always
It seems the launch has been successful,	remarkably
beyond our wildest dreams in fact. We are delighted	obviously
and we have had a large order from a company	already
in China. This is fabulous news. See you soon.	absolutely

C Describing the rate of change

How would you describe the sales growth of the items below?

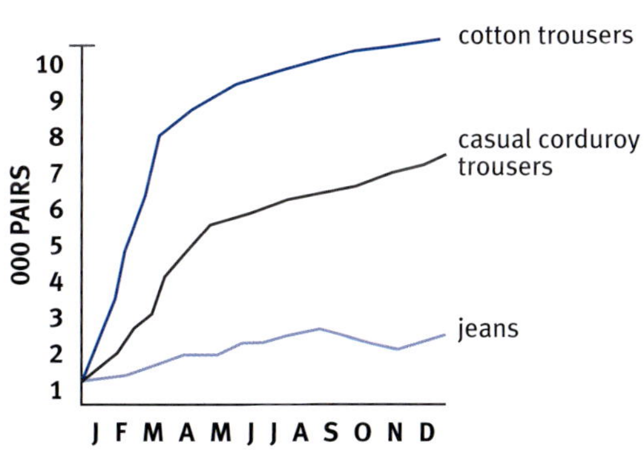

ADVERB POSITION AND USES (2)

USES

4 Changing focus and emphasis

The position of adverbs in a sentence is often flexible. This enables the speaker to make changes of focus and emphasis. The following are the common positions according to their function. For reasons of emphasis these positions may on occasion be different.

a) at the beginning of the sentence

OPINION	**In actual fact** I think she's wrong.
	Hopefully the situation will get better.
	Fortunately the damage was slight.
TIME	**A year ago** they decided to go public.
	To date we have received 321 requests for information.
	Originally the firm used to produce horseshoes.

b) in the middle of the sentence

MANNER	Prices could **suddenly** rise.
FREQUENCY	They **never** pay on time.
	I **occasionally** read *The Economist*.
OPINION	Her work record is **quite honestly** awful.
TIME	I am **still** waiting for permission.
	We have **already** sold over 50,000 units.
	Have you **ever** been to Finland?

c) at the end of the sentence

MANNER	I think the presentation went **well**.
	He works **fast**.
PLACE	She has never been **there**.
	You'll find him working **downstairs**.
TIME	The board talked about the share flotation **yesterday**.
	We'll have the prototype ready **soon**.
	I haven't seen Mr Khomsi **lately**.

5 Order

If there are a number of adverbs in the same sentence the order is usually:

1) Manner 2) Place 3) Time

We went to Madrid last month. (NOT *last month to Madrid)

They negotiated aggressively for four hours. (NOT *for four hours aggressively)

PRACTICE

A Commenting on the situation

Match the sentences in column A with those in column B.

A

1 It was his first real job interview for three years.
2 He missed the bus and thought he would be late.
3 During the interview they asked him why he wanted to work for their firm.
4 They said, 'Don't contact us, we'll contact you.'
5 He then did a course on interview skills.
6 He got to know a lot of famous musicians and went on tour with them.

B

a) **Eventually**, he set up his own label and became a millionaire.
b) **Shortly after**, he managed to find a job with a major record label.
c) **Luckily**, someone gave him a lift and he got there on time.
d) **Naturally**, he felt very nervous.
e) **Foolishly**, he said that he just needed the money and any job would do.
f) **Obviously**, he hadn't got the job.

B Your situation

Using an appropriate adverb, respond to these questions about your own work situation, as in the example.

EXAMPLE:

How quickly do your colleagues work? *They work extremely fast.*

1 Do they ever arrive late for work?
2 Where do you usually work?
3 How well do you get on with your boss?
4 Have you seen him or her recently?
5 What do you think of his / her performance? (be honest)

C Adverb position

Insert the adverbs into each line of this message in the most natural position.

Thank you for the e-mail you sent *yesterday*. I have spoken to Eric	yesterday; already
but he says he is waiting for confirmation from the board	still
before we can go ahead with the proposed changes. The delay	quite frankly
is getting on my nerves but I hope to get started on the project.	very soon
As is the case, we will receive confirmation at the last	often; suddenly
minute and have to work for the next couple of months	flat out
in order to get into production.	fast

UNIT 11

Nouns (identifying people and things)

NOUN FORMATION

We use some words only as nouns: *car*, *shelf*, *strategy*, etc. In other cases, nouns can be derived from other words, notably from verbs by adding a suffix. For example:

deliver → deliver**y**	employ → employ**ment**	exhibit → exhibit**ion**

Some of the common noun endings are:

depart → depart**ure**	initiate → initiat**ive**	perform → perform**ance**
promote → promot**ion**	recruit → recruit**ment**	refer → refer**ence**
store → stor**age**	train → train**ing**	

Nouns can also be formed from adjectives or other nouns:

accurate → accura**cy**	capital → capital**ism**	effective → effective**ness**
free → free**dom**	partner → partner**ship**	reliable → reliabil**ity**

Some nouns have the same form as verbs. For example:

attempt benefit blame budget call claim copy cost delay
help lack offer share supply support try wait walk wish

Sometimes the pronunciation is different, even though the noun and the verb have the same form:

Verb	*Noun*	*Verb*	*Noun*
con 'duct	'conduct	pro 'duce	'produce
dis 'count	'discount	re 'cord	'record
in 'crease	'increase	re 'ject	'reject
ob 'ject	'object	sub 'ject	'subject
per 'mit	'permit	trans 'fer	'transfer

Activities

A frequent way of forming nouns is by adding *-ing* to a verb. In this way, we can refer to an action, activity or process in a general way. The noun or noun phrase may be the subject or the object of the verb:

Training is essential for a flexible labour force.
Making money is not everything in life.

She has to do a lot of **entertaining**.
More has to be done to prevent **counterfeiting**.

People

Nouns referring to people can be formed with *-er*, *-or*, *-ian*, *-ee*, *-ant* and *-ist*:

lawy**er**	audit**or**	music**ian**	employ**ee**	assist**ant**	dent**ist**
report**er**	realt**or**	technic**ian**	train**ee**	consult**ant**	scient**ist**

PRACTICE

A Noun formation

Using a dictionary if necessary, complete the two columns with words derived from the verbs and adjectives given. Use the suffixes on the opposite page.

Verb	*Noun*	*Adjective*	*Noun*
accept	....	aware	....
agree	....	complex	....
counterfeit	....	creative (2 answers)	....
enter (2 answers)	....	effective	....
initiate	....	prosperous	....
occur	....	punctual	....
protect	....	real (2 answers)	....
race (2 answers)	....	reliable	....
refer	....	social (2 answers)	....
store	....	weak	....
waste	....	wise	....

B Activities

Match the sentence halves.

1 Flying on a charter flight
2 Reducing poverty and homelessness
3 Making a profit for the shareholders
4 Speaking in front of a large audience
5 Setting up a joint venture abroad
6 Headhunting

a) is the primary aim of most businesses.
b) is a way of breaking into an export market.
c) is a priority for the new left-wing government.
d) is an effective method of recruiting key executives.
e) can be a stressful experience.
f) is cheaper than on a scheduled one.

C People

Complete each sentence with a noun that refers to the type of person described.

1 He works at the reception so he's a ....
2 A contract is signed by both the employer and the ....
3 He works in the legal department so he's a ....
4 As an ...., she audits the company's accounts.
5 She works in real estate so she's a ....
6 She studied electricity and became an ....
7 As a .... for the *Financial Times*, he reports on events around the world.
8 As a freelance ...., he can sell his photos to newspapers and magazines.
9 Over 200 people applied for the job we advertised; we didn't expect so many ....

TYPES OF NOUN

Nouns belong to two broad families: *countable nouns* and *uncountable nouns*.

Countable nouns include:

- individual things, people and places:
  a diary   a memo   a photo   a receptionist   a factory   a corridor
- units of measurement:
  a metre   a mile   a kilo   a pound   a litre   a gallon

Countable nouns:

- are used with *a / an*
- can be used in the plural (diaries, memos, etc.)
- follow words such as *many, these, those, several, few, a few, a number of*

Uncountable nouns include:

- substances:
  gas   glass   gold   iron   oil   plastic   water
- many abstract ideas:
  access   freedom   health   humour   profitability   progress   relevance   safety
- verbal nouns:
  brainstorming   coaching   job-sharing   restructuring   timing

Uncountable nouns:

- do not take *the* when used in a general sense (NOT *the travel broadens the mind)
- take the singular form of the verb
- have words like *much, a little, little, some, a great deal of* before them

Some of the more common uncountable nouns are:

accommodation   advertising   advice   baggage   cash   clothing   damage
employment   equipment   finance   furniture   hardware   information
insurance   legislation   merchandise   money   news   progress   research
software   traffic   training   transport   travel   weather   work

We can use a countable expression to refer to an uncountable noun, e.g. a type of accommodation, a piece of advice:

accommodation: a place to live

advice: a piece of advice

training: a training course

work: a job / task

advertising: an advertisement

information: a piece of information

insurance: an insurance policy

PRACTICE

A Countable or uncountable?

Decide whether the following nouns are used as countable nouns (C) or uncountable nouns (U), as in the examples.

She has had three years' **experience** as a solicitor. ......U......

The demotion was a painful **experience**. ......C......

1 Are you here for **business** or pleasure? ....
2 He has set up a small fashion **business**. ....
3 I've never read the **works** of Shakespeare. ....
4 She's found **work** as a commercial assistant. ....
5 Have you got a good **light** in your study? ....
6 Were you able to throw any **light** on the subject? ....
7 We'll need some more wine **glasses** for the reception. ....
8 Fifty per cent of our bottles are made of recycled **glass**. ....
9 They failed to reach an **agreement**. ....
10 Is there **agreement** on how much will be spent? ....
11 We need to buy some new office **equipment**. ....
12 Apprentices have to build a piece of **equipment** as part of the course's learning outcomes. ....

B Matching countable and uncountable nouns

Match each countable noun with an uncountable noun with a similar meaning.

traffic equipment insurance machines accidents cars employment policies travel advice news laws legislation damage jobs journey bulletins hints

Countable	*Uncountable*
....	....
....	....
....	....
....	....
....	....
....	....
....	....
....	....
....	....

PLURAL NOUNS

We add *-s* to form the plural of most nouns. If the noun ends in *-s*, *-x*, *-ch* or *-sh*, we add *-es*:

box**es** church**es** class**es** crash**es** watch**es**

We also add *-es* to the following:

hero → hero**es** potato → potato**es** tomato → tomato**es**

If the final consonant of a noun is followed by *-y*, it is changed into *-ies*:

delivery → deliver**ies** party → part**ies** worry → worr**ies**

There are nouns which only occur in the plural. For example:

Earnings per share have increased.

The **goods** will be sent by special delivery.

I'm getting fat and my **trousers** are too tight.

We've opened new **premises** in Warsaw.

He lives on the **outskirts** of the town.

What **means** of transport do you prefer?

Their **headquarters** are in Boston.

Don't leave **valuables** in your car.

All her **clothes** were lost at the airport.

Refreshments are available in the lobby.

Many **thanks** for your invitation.

Works Entrance

Singular nouns ending in *-s*

Some nouns end in *-s* but are not plural:

The **news** was good.

Economics is not an exact science.

Politics has never been one of my favourite subjects.

The only **means** of communication was sign language.

Irregular plurals

Some words do not take an *-s* but have other endings or stay the same:

aircraft → aircraft criterion → criteria foot → feet formula → formulae (or formulas)
half → halves life → lives matrix → matrices person → people phenomenon → phenomena
tooth → teeth woman → women

Groups and organisations

Singular nouns such as *bank* or *committee* can be seen either as a number of people (plural) or as a collective unit (singular). As a result, the verb or pronoun that follows may be either singular or plural.

The bank **has** sent me my new credit card.

The committee **have** shelved the project.

Other words in this category include:

club firm government management media police public staff team union

Companies are often treated as singular:

General Electric **has** announced **its** new CEO.

PRACTICE

A Nouns only occurring in the plural

Complete the sentences using these words.

refreshments	premises	valuables	goods	works	crossroads	outskirts	means

1 Their offices are on the .... of Milan.

2 The money was acquired by dishonest ....

3 Please hand in all .... to the reception desk.

4 The demand for .... and services is lower this year.

5 Our new .... are located downtown near the municipal library.

6 He's the official in charge of the engineering ....

7 .... – tea, coffee and snacks – will be served during the break.

8 When I became redundant for the first time, I felt I had reached a .... in my life.

B Making nouns plural

What is the plural of the following words?

1 bag
2 person
3 party
4 formula
5 potato
6 shelf
7 fax
8 knife
9 criterion
10 match

C Singular or plural?

Complete the sentences with *is*, *are*, *has* or *have*.

1 Statistics .... a subject about which I know very little.

2 The goods you ordered .... arrived.

3 All their belongings .... in their hotel room.

4 People .... often strange.

5 Mathematics .... often used as a test of intelligence.

6 The government .... a new piece of legislation to introduce.

D Common mistakes

Correct the errors in these sentences.

1 The news are bad, I'm afraid.

2 She knows a great many persons.

3 Stress at work is not a recent phenomena.

4 Our office is situated in a pleasant surrounding.

5 The staffs are unhappy with the new arrangements.

TWO NOUNS TOGETHER

There are three main ways of putting two nouns together:

1 **noun + 's + noun**
the president's decision
the agent's fee

2 **noun + preposition + noun**
the punishment of fraud
an article on the theatre

3 **compound nouns**
a market survey
consumer confidence

1 Noun + *'s* + noun

We use the *'s* structure to express the relationships between nouns:

possession: John**'s** briefcase, Mr Smith**'s** office

relationships: my wife**'s** name, his brother**'s** success

duration and time: a month**'s** holiday, yesterday**'s** papers, this year**'s** results

's can be used to show that something belongs to or is associated with a place or an organisation:

New York**'s** Fifth Avenue Amsterdam**'s** canals Moscow**'s** Red Square

the board**'s** decision the company**'s** profits the bank**'s** important clients

's is added to a noun that specifies a part of an object or a quality it has:

the car**'s** design the computer**'s** memory the plane**'s** wing

2 Noun + *of* + noun

When we want to talk about a particular unit of something, we use a countable noun before an uncountable noun linked by *of*. For example:

a piece of equipment an item of news a piece of paper a piece of software

a plot of land a bit of trouble a bit of research a run of bad luck

Some constructions are relatively fixed combinations:

a word of advice a show of strength a spell of bad weather

a mountain of work a round of talks/negotiations a stroke of luck

Expressions of measurement follow this pattern:

a gallon of petrol a pint of beer a kilo of rice

The *of* structure is used to refer to containers and their contents. The noun + noun structure refers to the container without its contents:

a barrel of oil	an oil barrel	a packet of cigarettes	a cigarette packet
a jar of coffee	a coffee jar	a glass of wine	a wine glass

We also use an *of* structure with words that indicate a part of something:

the middle of the meeting the bottom of the page the back of the building the end of my stay

3 Compound nouns

A compound noun is a noun that is made up of two or more words. Many compound nouns in English are formed by nouns modified by other nouns. The first noun describes the second noun, telling us what kind of object or person it is or what its purpose is.

cash flow departure lounge filing cabinet mail box

PRACTICE

A Famous places

Match the place name and the feature it is famous for.

Copenhagen Berlin canals Madrid London Venice mermaid

New York Cairo skyscrapers Prado Brandenburg Gate pyramids Big Ben

EXAMPLE: Copenhagen's mermaid

B Amounts and quantities

Match an expression 1–6 with the appropriate noun a–f.

1 a lump of	a) coffee
2 a can of	b) salt
3 a jar of	c) beer
4 a bar of	d) toothpaste
5 a tube of	e) chocolate
6 a grain of	f) sugar

C Noun + *of* + noun

Study the entries from the *Longman Business English Dictionary* and complete the sentences below.

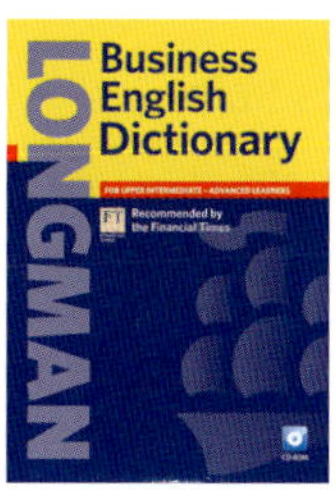

ˌrate of reˈturn plural **rates of return** [C] ACCOUNTING FINANCE the amount of profit that a particular investment will make, expressed as a percentage: *a guaranteed rate of return of 7%.*

ˌbasket of ˈcurrencies *n* plural **baskets of currencies** [C usually singular] FINANCE a group of currencies against which the value of another currency is measured: *The yen's exchange rate against a basket of currencies has fallen to its lowest level for three months.* –see also MARKET BASKET

ˌbreach of ˈcontract *n* plural **breaches of contract** [C,U] LAW when someone fails to do something that they have agreed to do in a contract: *Watson had to pay more than £55 million in damages for breach of contract.* | *Their tactic was to say that all striking drivers were* ***in breach of contract****, and fire them.*

ˌletter of ˈcredit written abbreviation **l/c** *n* plural **letters of credit** [C] FINANCE **1** in foreign trade, a written promise by an importer's bank to pay the exporter's bank on a particular date or at a particular time after the goods are sent by the exporter: *Coffee buyers in Central America are required to have proof of financing, such as a letter of credit.*

ˌconflict of ˈinterest *n* plural **conflicts of interest** [C,U] a situation in which you cannot do your job fairly because you have the power to decide something in a way that would be to your advantage, although this may not be the best decision: *There is a growing conflict of interest between her position as a politician and her business activities.*

1 Beijing has proposed the eventual replacement of the US dollar as the global reserve currency by a .... and commodities.

2 Her refusal to work flexible hours constituted a ....

3 We would expect a .... of at least 15% on our investment.

4 Being both a member of parliament and CEO of a major firm could lead to a ....

5 The bank has opened and confirmed an irrevocable .... in your favour.

COMPOUND NOUNS

1 Nouns used as adjectives

In the noun + noun structure, the first noun functions like an adjective and describes the second noun. Very often, the first noun answers the question *What kind?*

a bank transfer (a kind of transfer)
a bank loan (a kind of loan)
work experience (a kind of experience)
a work permit (a kind of permit)

We can also make compound nouns when the first noun ends in *-ing*:

the training budget a spending review a turning point

2 Singular with a plural meaning

In a compound noun the first noun is usually singular, even if it has a plural meaning:

a food store (a store that sells food)
a toolbox (a box that contains tools)
a car factory (a factory that produces cars)

Nouns in numerical expressions are always singular:

a four-star hotel a five-year plan a 35-hour week
a 50-dollar bill a ten-ton truck a million-dollar loan

However, the *s* is kept on the first noun in the following expressions:

accounts department clothes store customs officer futures market goods train
incomes policy needs analysis overseas branch savings account sports car
sales policy works manager

3 Choice of structures

Sometimes only one construction is possible:

a breach of contract (NOT *a contract's breach, a breach contract)
the terms of reference (NOT *reference terms, terms' reference)
Peter's friends (NOT *the friends of Peter, Peter friends)
a traffic jam (NOT *a traffic's jam, a jam's traffic, the traffic of jam)
a silicon chip (NOT *a silicon's chip, a chip's silicon, a chip of silicon)

Sometimes it is possible to use two structures but it is not possible to use all three:

the decision of the board / the board's decision (NOT *the board decision)
the responsibilities of the project manager /
  the project manager's responsibilities (NOT *the project manager responsibilities)

PRACTICE

A Noun combinations

One word can be used each time to make compound nouns, as in the example.

EXAMPLE:

answer ......phone......	......phone...... card	......phone...... number

1	.... pitch	.... figures	.... hype
2	savings	bank	.... number
3	bear	.... leader	home ....
4	.... awareness	.... image	.... loyalty
5	.... concessions	.... secret	.... union

B Choice of structures

Tick (✓) the correct expressions and cross (✗) the incorrect expressions, as in the examples.

EXAMPLES:

a point of view ✓

a viewpoint ✓

a view's point ✗

1 a window of opportunity
2 an opportunity's window
3 a promise's breach
4 a breach of promise
5 a sales target
6 a target of sales
7 data collection
8 data's collection
9 a needs analysis
10 a need analysis
11 a spending review
12 a review of spending
13 a spending's review
14 an eight-hour day
15 an eight hours day
16 an eight hours' day
17 a plant of recycling
18 a recycling plant

C Compound nouns

Use these words to make compound nouns and complete the text.

figures	sense	loyalty	revenue	production	~~operas~~

Soap ....operas.... are the economic powerhouses of television .... [1]. They are cheap to make and enjoy high viewing .... [2]. And the income is secure. They tend to run forever and the stars are not paid a lot for the time they spend on screen. They make good business .... [3] for broadcasters for they act as a focal point for the audience, building up viewer .... [4] and attracting advertising .... [5].

NOUNS AND PREPOSITIONS

1 Noun + preposition

Look at these noun + preposition combinations:

The English do not put the same resources into language teaching as others, and since the 17th century there has never been any particular **interest in** foreign languages.

Internal reorganisation was cited as the main **reason for** redundancies by 49.8% of the organisations surveyed.

The insurance industry last week published a code of practice on genetics. It says companies will seek medical **advice on** how to interpret tests.

Here is a list of nouns and the prepositions that follow them:

the alternative **to** job cuts	interest **in** my idea	a rise **in** prices
attention **to** detail	a need **for** change	a rise **of** 5%
an application **for** a grant	an order **for** goods	the solution **to** the problem
a cheque **for** £2,000	access **to** information	a tax **on** cigarettes
value **for** money	a request **for** more time	a fall **in** demand
a fall **of** 3%	the return **on** investment	a vote **of** confidence

2 Prepositional phrases

Prepositional phrases are formed when a noun follows a preposition. All the phrases below are common:

at:	your disposal our expense a profit/loss your risk short notice
beyond:	our control reasonable doubt our wildest dreams
by:	accident law mistake
in:	advance arrears bulk demand debt force due course full good condition stock transit
on:	approval arrival closer inspection delivery display loan a regular basis request sale schedule
out of:	date order stock work
through:	the usual channels no fault of our own
under:	pressure review separate cover way construction
within:	a week the next few months easy reach reason the budget

PRACTICE

A Which preposition?

Complete the sentences with a suitable preposition.

1 Thank you for your interest .... our proposal.
2 There has been a fall .... demand for their products.
3 There has been a fall .... 2.5% in the volume of sales.
4 What was the reason .... his resignation?
5 The government is increasing the tax .... cigarettes.
6 I made out a cheque .... 300 euros.
7 She is meticulous and pays great attention .... detail.
8 Plans are .... way for a new link road.

B Prepositional phrases

Use one preposition to complete each set of three sentences.

1 The error was due to circumstances .... our control.
It started off good-humouredly but then went .... a joke.
Roger Penrose is, ... a doubt, one of the great minds of our time.

2 .... law, you have to carry an identity card in many countries.
I met her quite .... chance in the street in Munich.
Someone left the door open .... mistake.

3 I will be in touch .... due course.
We're .... luck; there's still one left.
The debt must be paid .... full by 31 January.

4 Mr Evans will meet you .... your arrival.
I don't always use the car; I try to go .... foot whenever possible.
The goods seemed all right but .... closer inspection at least 30% were defective.

5 Mrs Gonzales cannot see you .... such short notice.
A chauffeur-driven car will be put .... your disposal.
I attended the reception .... the chairperson's invitation.

UNIT 12

Identifying nouns

ARTICLES (*a/an*, *the* and zero article)

FORM We use *a* when the next word begins with a consonant sound and *an* when it begins with a vowel sound.

a bill a European a house a magazine a union
an ability an estimate an hour an MBA an umbrella

USES Uses of *a* / *an*, *the* and zero article (Ø)

a / an

1 Before unspecified singular countable nouns:

He lives in **a** flat. (we don't know anything else about it)

2 Before professions:

She's **a** chemical engineer and he's **a** project manager.

3 In expressions of measurement:

The speed limit is 55 miles **an** hour.

It costs €1.35 **a** litre.

4 To describe 'all examples of the same kind':

A balance sheet is **a** document that lists assets and liabilities.

the

5 Before a specific noun that we have mentioned before:

I had a BMW and a Mercedes but I sold **the** BMW to my brother.

6 When it is clear what particular thing or place is meant:

I'll meet you in **the** staff car park behind **the** warehouse. Where is **the** restroom?

7 When two nouns are joined with *of*:

the history **of** commerce **the** balance **of** trade

8 Before adjectives to specify a category of people or things:

the rich **the** poor **the** middle classes **the** mobile phone (a type of phone)
the textile industry

9 Before some institutions:

the United Nations **the** IMF **the** Bundesbank **the** BBC

10 In superlative expressions:

Toyota is **the** biggest car manufacturer.

zero article

11 With uncountable nouns used in a general sense:

Nothing succeeds like (**Ø**) success.
(**Ø**) Unity is (**Ø**) strength. (**Ø**) Information is (**Ø**) power.

12 Before unspecified plural nouns:

(**Ø**) People often distrust (**Ø**) politicians.

13 Before the names of places and people:

(**Ø**) Oxford (**Ø**) Singapore (**Ø**) Dr Schweitzer (**Ø**) President Lincoln

But note: **the** Kennedy family **the** King of Saudi Arabia

PRACTICE

A *a* / *an*, *the* and zero article

Read the following passage and identify the uses of *a* / *an*, *the* and zero article with each noun. Give them a number (1–13) which corresponds to one of the categories on the previous page.

My brother Michael used to be a **teacher** ..Category 2.. in a village **school** ..Category 1.. near **Cambridge** ....[1]. The **job** ....[2] was interesting but tiring and not very well-paid. He spent most of his free time on his hobby – collecting and repairing antique **clocks** ....[3]. Then he had an **idea** ....[4]. The **CBI** ....[5] (Confederation of British Industry) was helping **people** ....[6] start up by themselves. Why not go on a training **course** ....[7], apply for a **loan** ....[8] and set up a small **business** ....[9]?

So he resigned from the **school** ....[10], said goodbye to the **children** ....[11], and joined the **unemployed** ....[12]. He obtained **information** ....[13] from different **sources** ....[14], took **advice** ....[15] from an **accountant** ....[16], left the **village** ....[17] and learnt all about the antique **trade** ....[18]. Eighteen months later he had his own shop and was earning about £2,000 a **month** ....[19]. 'It was the best **thing** ....[20] I ever did,' he says.

B Ferrari

Complete the blanks with *a* / *an*, *the* or Ø.

..Ø.. Enzo Ferrari's death in August 1988 was ....[1] sad occasion. However, it did release ....[2] company from ....[3] grip of his idiosyncratic ways and enabled ....[4] firm to move into ....[5] new era.

....................[6] appointment of Luca di Montezemolo in December 1991 was ....[7] beginning of ....[8] series of ....[9] changes. His aim was to invest in ....[10] research and ....[11] development and to bridge ....[12] gap between ....[13] racing and production car businesses. He also introduced ....[14] sponsorship, although ....[15] constructor still has fewer names on its cars than ....[16] other teams. ....[17] CEO is steering ....[18] narrow course between modernising ....[19] company while trying to avoid diluting ....[20] mystique that makes ....[21] brand so great.

Enzo Ferrari

Luca di Montezemolo

QUANTIFIERS (1)

USES

1 Talking about unspecific amounts

We use *some* with both plural countable nouns or uncountable nouns to talk about a quantity or number without being very precise:

Some people are workaholics.

Operating profits were **some** £180m.

Would you like **some** coffee?

Some analysts are saying that the crisis will continue for **some** time.

We use *any* most commonly in negative sentences and in questions to talk about a quantity of something that may or may not exist:

Have you **any** baggage with you?

There isn't **any** time left.

We haven't got **any** components in stock.

Do you have **any** tickets for the concert?

2 Talking about total amounts

Any can indicate that *all* examples of the noun are to be included:

Any manager will tell you that good organisation is important. (= all managers)

An e-mail can be received at **any** time of the day or night. (= 24 hours a day)

Choose **any** model you like. (= it doesn't matter which model)

All and *all of* are both possible before a noun with a determiner:

He's taken **all** (**of**) the paper.

If there is no determiner, we do not use *of* with a plural countable noun:

All formal meetings are a waste of time in his opinion. (NOT *all of meetings)

Note that *all* does not go between *the* and a noun:

He spent the **whole** meeting looking at his watch. (NOT *the all meeting)

3 Zero quantities

No and *none of* mean 'not any' and 'not one':

We've had **no** complaints about our services. (= we have not received any)

They have paid **none of** their invoices. (= not one)

None of the initial ideas was / were accepted.

PRACTICE

A Amounts

Complete the sentences using *some*, *any*, *no* or *none*.

1 We haven't had .... news from our agent.
2 I have absolutely .... idea what he wants.
3 The deal was worth .... $16 billion.
4 .... of his proposals were very good.
5 .... of his proposals was very good.
6 He has .... very old bottles of wine in his cellar.
7 We employ people of .... race, religion or ethnic origin.
8 There is .... point in wasting .... more time on this issue.
9 I am enclosing .... information about our range of products.
10 'Have you got .... extra leaflets?' 'Sorry, there are .... left.'
11 My new car uses hardly .... petrol at all compared to my previous one.
12 .... ill-advised people try to get by in Japan without hiring a good interpreter.

B A letter of complaint

Complete the letter with *all*, *some*, *any*, *no* or *none*.

Dear Mr Andrews,

I am sending this letter by registered mail as ....[1] of my previous correspondence has received a reply.

You will recall from our agreement of 3 January this year that ....[2] delay in the delivery of essential components would be subject to a penalty clause. So far we have received ....[3] word from your plant manager that the components we ordered ....[4] weeks ago have been sent.

I would be grateful if you would take ....[5] the necessary steps to ensure that these components are received without ....[6] further delay. Otherwise we will have ....[7] option but to enforce the penalty clause in the contract.

Yours sincerely,

Proverb

You can fool all people some of the time and some people all of the time, but you can't fool all people all of the time.

QUANTIFIERS (2)

USES

4 Referring to large amounts

Much and *many* mean a large quantity or number of something. *Much* is used with uncountable nouns and *many* with countable ones:

Many decisions are made without **much** thought.

Did you meet **many** people at the conference?

We haven't made **much** progress recently.

How **much** money do you want to earn?

Both *many* and *much* can be replaced by *a lot of*. *Many* can be replaced by *a large number (of)* and *much* by *a great deal of*:

We stock **many** / **a large number of** spare parts in the warehouse.

We've spent **a great deal of** time on this project.

Note that we avoid using *much* in positive statements:

The fire did **a lot of** damage. (NOT *much damage)

5 Talking about limited amounts

A few and *some* are used with countable nouns to refer to a restricted quantity:

I like **a few** / **some** Australian wines but not all of them.

I've got **a few** minutes to spare.

A little and *some* are used with uncountable nouns:

I've got **a little** / **some** cash on me but not much.

A little can be used with adjectives to mean 'to a certain extent':

The size of the deficit was **a little** surprising.

A little and *a few* point in a positive direction; *little* and *few* are more negative:

He has (very) **little** initiative and always waits to be told what to do.

There is **little** we can do about it; we'll just have to wait and see.

Few employees enjoy being appraised.

(Very) **few** people read philosophy for pleasure.

6 Talking about excessive / insufficient amounts

We use *too* before adjectives and adverbs, and before *much*, *many*, *few* and *little*. We use *enough* after adjectives and adverbs, and before nouns.

She drives far **too** fast. I'm scared when I'm in a car with her.

I've never been trekking – it's probably **too** tiring and I'm **not** fit **enough**.

I haven't got **enough** money to buy a helicopter.

He didn't react quickly **enough**.

PRACTICE

A Correct the errors

Correct the errors in these sentences.

1 He didn't reply enough fast.
2 The flood caused many damage.
3 What she said was a few strange.
4 The whole process uses very few electricity.
5 I enjoyed few of her books but not all of them.
6 We haven't made many progress recently.
7 I don't think he has experience enough for the job.
8 She works mostly on her own so she has very little colleagues.
9 I've got few minutes to spare so we can continue if you like.
10 The final date for submission was three weeks ago so it's far enough late now.

B An e-mail

Complete the e-mail with these words. You will need to use one word twice.

little	few	much	too	a great deal	a little	a few	many	enough

SEND From: LC

ATTACH To: Malcolm Bridgewater

Subject: Sales & promotion

Sales figures for the year to date have been .... [1] disappointing as .... [2] distributors are willing to promote our products as .... [3] as we would like. The commission is relatively low and therefore there is very .... [4] incentive for them to ensure volume sales. This said, sales of some lines have done better in the run-up to Christmas.

We recently did a survey of 1,500 customers. Unfortunately, very .... [5] of those questioned (7%) said that our designs were attractive and .... [6] people (over half of the respondents) felt they were far .... [7] old-fashioned. As a result I have commissioned a new design and spent .... [8] of time with the marketing department. I am sending you .... [9] samples for you to comment on and, if they are good .... [10], we can start using them in the New Year.

UNIT 13 Describing nouns

ADJECTIVES

FORM

Many adjectives are not derived from other words:

old new high low rich poor hard soft

However, you can recognise many adjectives from their endings. The word the adjective is derived from is either a noun or a verb. Here is a list of the most common endings, together with nouns that the adjectives often combine with:

-able:	adjustable seatbelt	profitable venture	workable arrangement
-al:	professional image	international dimension	promotional literature
-ant:	important decision	pleasant meal	dominant partner
-ary:	monetary policy	supplementary benefit	voluntary redundancy
-ed:	limited company	contented customer	vested interest
-ent:	confident manner	convenient time	independent survey
-ful:	successful career	careful planning	fruitful discussion
-ial:	industrial sabotage	judicial enquiry	potential disaster
-ible:	deductible income	legible handwriting	negligible amount
-ic:	economic policy	realistic forecast	strategic acquisition
-ing:	convincing argument	leading brand	boring meeting
-ive:	competitive salary	exclusive distributor	positive outlook
-less:	endless discussion	hopeless case	useless idea
-ly:	costly mistake	quarterly statement	timely intervention
-ous:	ambitious politician	famous actor	tremendous increase
-y:	busy employee	risky venture	wealthy banker

Forming opposites

We often use prefixes such as *dis-*, *il-*, *im-*, *in-*, *ir-*, *mis-* and *un-* to say that something is *not* the case:

dis-:	dishonest	disorganised	dissatisfied
il-:	illegal	illegible	illicit
im-:	impatient	impossible	impractical
in-:	inaccurate	incompetent	informal
ir-:	irregular	irrevocable	irrecoverable
mis-:	mismanaged	misinformed	mistaken
un-:	uneconomic	unfashionable	unsuccessful

PRACTICE

A Your personal profile

The personal profile grid can help you reveal your personality! Place a tick (✓) in the boxes next to the five words that describe you best. Put a cross (✗) next to the five words that describe you least.

persuasive	☐	original	☐	dutiful	☐	pleasant	☐
cheerful	☐	loyal	☐	courageous	☐	happy	☐
competitive	☐	sociable	☐	considerate	☐	playful	☐
submissive	☐	inspiring	☐	adventurous	☐	talkative	☐
conventional	☐	decisive	☐	impatient	☐	diplomatic	☐
aggressive	☐	cautious	☐	determined	☐	responsible	☐
restless	☐	pioneering	☐	nonchalant	☐	ambitious	☐

B Adjective formation

Complete the job reference with the correct form of the words in brackets.

As requested, this is a reference for Ms Wright, who spent four years working in my department.

Becker plc is a highly .... [1] (success) company specialising in precision .... [2] (science) instruments in a highly .... [3] (compete) market. During her time with Becker, Ms Wright was .... [4] (responsibility) for translating .... [5] (promotion) literature into English. This work requires someone who is .... [6] (autonomy) and capable of producing .... [7] (accuracy) translations of both sales information and .... [8] (technique) documentation. Ms Wright proved to be an extremely .... [9] (competence) and .... [10] (loyalty) employee. I fully recommend her for the position.

COMPOUND ADJECTIVES

FORM

1 Two-word adjectives

Many adjectives are formed by joining two (or more) words with a hyphen (-). There are many types of combinations:

adj + noun:	a **small-scale** operation, a **long-term** policy
adj + noun + *-ed*:	a **narrow-minded** approach, a **short-sighted** policy
adj or adv + past participle:	**low-paid** workers, a **well-informed** person
adj, adv, noun + present participle:	a **high-flying** professional, a **far-reaching** effect, a **record-breaking** year, a **problem-solving** approach
noun + adj:	a **tax-free** salary, a **brand-new** product

A few compound adjectives consist of three words:

the **day-to-day** organisation	**up-to-date** information
an **out-of-court** settlement	a **down-to-earth** approach

2 Prefixes and suffixes

Some prefixes and suffixes have productive uses; they can combine with many other words to form new words. Here are just a few:

extra-:	extra-large	extra-soft	extra-special
self-:	self-defeating	self-imposed	self-regulating
well-:	well-attended	well-known	well-respected
-based:	London-based	city-based	overseas-based
-minded:	open-minded	like-minded	single-minded
-oriented:	market-oriented	consumer-oriented	export-oriented
-rich:	asset-rich	cash-rich	oil-rich

3 Adjectives + nouns

Some adjectives are frequently found with certain nouns and form a relatively fixed word partnership:

We have a **joint account** at the bank.

After a **heated discussion** he stormed out of the meeting.

We're facing **keen competition** from cheap imports.

The outcome was a **foregone conclusion**; everyone knew what would happen.

The biggest **stumbling block** to a peace settlement is the disputed frontier.

Profit-sharing gives everybody a **vested interest** in the company's success.

They say they would use force only as a **last resort**.

PRACTICE

A Compound adjectives

Use one word to complete each of these sets of expressions.

1 trouble-.................... maintenance
tax-.................... salary
interest-.................... credit

2 ....-service restaurant
....................-drive car
....................-defeating policy

3 single-.................... approach
narrow-.................... attitude
serious-.................... student

4 ....-educated employees
....................-established firm
....................-attended meeting

5 short-.................... contract
medium-.................... investment
long-.................... policy

6 ....-flying professional
....................-risk strategy
....................-speed train

B Adjectives and nouns

Match the words on the left with those on the right to form word partnerships. Then complete the sentences below.

1 foregone	a) interest
2 joint	b) priority
3 last	c) exchange
4 heated	d) account
5 stumbling	e) conclusion
6 high	f) competition
7 stiff	g) resort
8 vested	h) block

1 We won the contract in the face of ....
2 My wife and I have a .... at the National Bank.
3 After a .... of views we agreed to disagree.
4 Companies are giving .... to risks related to climate change.
5 As a .... we could sell some assets but only if all else fails.
6 The territorial dispute is the main .... to a peace agreement.
7 There was no point in having a discussion because the outcome was a ....
8 The tobacco industry has a .... in claiming that smoking does not damage health.

ADJECTIVE POSITION

FORM Adjectives can be used in two positions – before nouns and after verbs such as *be*, *become*, *seem* and *appear*:

a **high** price	The price seemed **high**.
a **famous** writer	The writer became **famous**.
an **impossible** situation	The situation appeared **impossible**.
an **obvious** solution	The solution was **obvious**.

Most adjectives can be used in both ways. However, some can be used in one way only.

1 Adjectives only used before the noun

The **former** chairperson was forced to resign.

We only give extended credit as a **last** resort.

The **main** thing is not to worry.

A **joint** venture with an overseas firm can be a **major** advantage.

The **previous** agreement was signed in December 1999.

2 Adjectives used after the noun

In the following examples it would be incorrect to put the adjective before the noun:

The funds **allocated** to the project did not cover the expenditure.

The people **questioned** during the survey thought the packaging was good.

The issues **discussed** during the meeting were all resolved.

I'd like to refer to one of the points **raised** during the last meeting.

The goods **ordered** last month have not yet been delivered.

The warning **issued** by the authorities was ignored.

In each of the above examples, *who were* or *which were* could be inserted:

The funds (which were) **allocated** to the project did not cover the expenditure.

The people (who were) **questioned** during the survey thought the packaging was good.

3 Adjectives used in both positions but with a change of meaning

the **present** members of the committee (= those who are members now)

the members of the committee **present** (= those in attendance)

She holds an extremely **responsible** post. (= needing ability and sound judgement)

He is **responsible** for sales in South East Asia. (= is in charge of)

She gave us a long, **involved** explanation. (= complicated)

There is a lot of documentation **involved** in getting a government loan. (= connected)

He is an **outstanding** candidate for the post. (= exceptional)

There are a number of invoices **outstanding**. (= unpaid)

PRACTICE

A Which adjective?

Complete the sentences with these adjectives.

last	major	former	obvious	present	previous

1 Lady Thatcher is a .... British prime minister.
2 This is the .... time I make excuses for him.
3 The .... decision was overturned by the committee.
4 In the .... situation it's better to act without delay.
5 The high value of the pound was a .... problem for British exporters.
6 The company representative will be ....; she'll be wearing a red uniform.

B Before or after the noun?

Which of the phrases in *italics* is correct?

1 The *discussed issues / issues discussed* have not been solved.
2 The *money allocated / allocated money* to the project did not cover costs.
3 I'd like to go back to one of the *raised points / points raised* by Mr Collins.
4 The *uniform issued / issued uniform* has not been returned.
5 The *ordered goods / goods ordered* have finally arrived.
6 The *women questioned / questioned women* during the survey thought the perfume smelt good.
7 She is an exceptional woman of *outstanding ability / ability outstanding*.
8 I don't want to enter into a long, *involved argument / argument involved* about who is to blame.

C Sentence rearrangement

The words in these sentences are in the wrong order. Rewrite them in the correct order.

1 the the statement by government issued misinterpreted was
2 the the problems during meeting solved have raised been
3 you shouldn't the worry main is thing that
4 me her an impossible to cooperate has refusal in situation put

ADJECTIVES AND ADVERBS

FORM

1 Adjectives usually describe nouns and adverbs modify verbs (see page 72):

Adjectives	*Adverbs*
She's a **good** driver.	She drives **well**.
We need an **immediate** answer.	We need an answer **immediately**.
She has a **soft** voice.	She speaks **softly**.

2 Some adjectives and adverbs have the same form:

He's a **fast** talker.	He talks **fast**. (NOT *fastly)
Mrs Dyke is a **hard** worker.	She works **hard**. (NOT *hardly)
There are **daily** flights.	Flights leave **daily**.
I have a **full** diary.	My diary looks **full**.
We need to make an **early** start.	We need to start **early**.

3 Some adjectives end in *-ly* but have no corresponding adverbs:

An electron microscope is a **costly** piece of equipment.

She's a very **friendly** person to work with.

We had a **lively** discussion about the origins of the universe.

I left the firm because of the **miserly** salary.

4 We can use adverbs to modify adjectives, past participles or other adverbs:

She speaks **extremely fast**.

Such a mistake is **easily made**.

He was wearing a **really colourful** tie.

Their business has been **hugely successful**.

A peaceful solution to the conflict is **increasingly unlikely**.

5 Some adjectives have two corresponding adverbs:

The train from Toledo was **late**.	We haven't seen each other **lately**. (= recently) The train arrived **late**.
Let me ask you a **direct** question.	His ideas are **directly** opposed to mine. Can we fly **direct** to Chicago?
There will be a **short** delay.	We hope to see you **shortly**. (= soon) Sales fell **short** of target.
Sorry. **Wrong** number.	I was **wrongly** dressed for a formal dinner. Why does everything go **wrong**?

PRACTICE

A Common mistakes

Tick (✓) the correct sentences. Correct the errors in the incorrect sentences.

1 She likes driving fast cars.
2 I work hardly because I am highly paid.
3 She's a very friendly person.
4 Everything I do recently seems to go wrongly.
5 We need to start earlily.
6 It could be a complex and costly procedure.
7 Time is running shortly.

B Adverb position

Complete the text appropriately with these adverbs.

increasingly	easily	extremely	unfortunately	hugely	deeply	suitably	awfully

TMP

If there is one certainty in life, it is that things change. And in the modern world things are changing .... [1] fast. This is especially true in the workplace where there is no longer the concept of a job for life. People are .... [2] likely to work for many different companies throughout their careers. It is .... [3] common – and .... [4] disturbing – for companies to say, 'Why should we train staff for them to leave for better jobs?' This is an .... [5] outmoded concept because staff will move, regardless of whether they receive training or not.

So how can individuals be .... [6] prepared to meet the challenges of change? This is not a question that can be .... [7] answered, but we at TMP Consultants believe we have developed some .... [8] successful recipes that will help you get the best out of your employees while they stay with you.

PREPOSITIONS OF PLACE AND DIRECTION

USES We use prepositions to say where a person or thing is, or their direction.

1 *about / around* (approximate position)

She's left her briefcase lying **about** somewhere. (she doesn't know exactly where)

2 *across* (from one side to the other)

He walked **across** the room and looked out of the window.

3 *at* (precise location)

He's sitting **at** his desk.

The British Prime Minister lives **at** 10 Downing Street.

4 *at* (direction)

Our campaign is aimed **at** the top end of the market.

What are you looking **at**?

5 *beyond* (limit in direction)

Warning! No unauthorised personnel **beyond** this point.

6 *by* (close to)

I can see him over there **by** the news stand.

7 *from* (source)

The cars are imported **from** Slovenia.

8 *in* (three-dimensional space)

He works **in** Frankfurt.

She puts everything **in** her handbag.

9 *on* (two-dimensional line or surface)

Paris stands **on** the River Seine.

A painting by Miro hangs **on** the boardroom wall.

10 *round / around* (after turning)

Go straight ahead and the bank is just **round / around** the corner.

11 *through* (direction between two points in space)

We drove **through** Baltimore on our way to Washington.

12 *to* (movement, destination)

I have to go **to** Prague next week.

A taxi will take you **to** the airport.

13 *up / down* (a place further along a path or road)

She's just gone **up / down** the road to the bank.

PRACTICE

A Which preposition?

Label each picture with its appropriate preposition.

1 

....

2 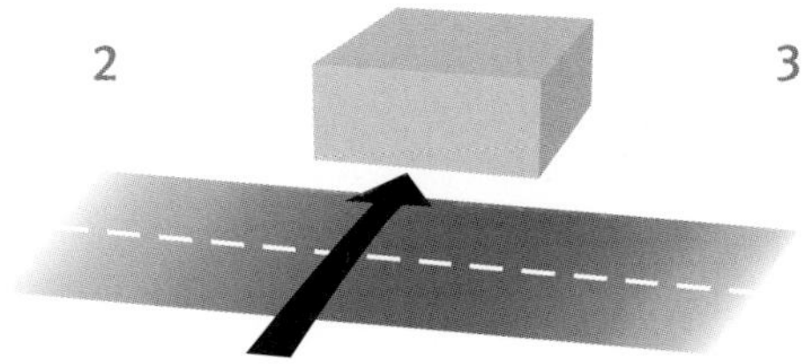

....

3 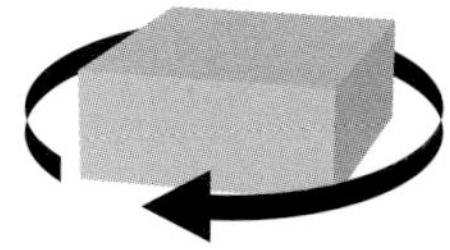

....

4 

....

5 

....

6 

....

7 

....

8 

....

B Sentence completion

Complete the sentences with an appropriate preposition.

1 Why is she always leaving her files lying ....?
2 Diamonds are imported .... South Africa.
3 He works .... the centre of the business district.
4 Cairo stands .... the River Nile.
5 You can't see it .... here but the theatre is just .... the corner.
6 We went .... Spain on our way .... France .... Portugal.
7 She's over there .... the coffee machine.
8 She lives .... Amsterdam but is moving .... The Hague soon.
9 The best restaurant is just .... the road.
10 From the top of the tower you can see the cathedral and the mountains ....

PREPOSITIONS OF TIME

USES We use prepositions to say when something happens.

1 *around / about* (approximately)

She'll get here **around** 11 o'clock.

2 *at* (point in time)

I'll pick you up **at** 2.30.

He takes work home **at** the weekend.

3 *beyond* (limit in duration)

It's impossible to extend credit **beyond** 30 days.

4 *by* (limit in time)

The plane leaves at 9 so we must be at the airport **by** 8am.

5 *from* (starting point in time)

The new procedure will be in operation **from** 1 January.

6 *in* (between two points in time)

The new museum was opened to the public **in** 2007. (some time in that year)

We got to the match **in** time to see the kick-off. (we arrived before and didn't miss anything)

They employ temps **in** the summer vacation.

Multimedia applications began to take off **in** the 1990s.

7 *on* (point of time)

My birthday is **on** 3 April.

Please arrive **on** time. (at exactly the right time, not late)

Our weekly planning meeting is **on** Monday morning.

8 *through* (direction inside time)

I'll be staying in Florida April **through** June. (American English)

She slept all **through** the meeting.

9 *to* (future direction)

It's two minutes **to** four.

There are only two weeks **to** the launch.

The store is open from 10 **to** 6.30 every day, except Sunday. (= until)

10 *until* (limit in time)

We have **until** the end of June to settle the debt.

I'll be staying in Florida from April **until** June.

PRACTICE

A Which preposition?

Complete the sentences with an appropriate preposition of time.

1 Easter falls .... 5 April this year.
2 He'll be back .... an hour's time.
3 He took copious notes all .... the meeting.
4 I'll see you .... 6 o'clock. Make sure you're .... time!
5 The government privatised massively .... the 1990s.
6 The financial year runs .... 1 April .... the following 31 March.
7 We arrived just .... time to see the opening ceremony.
8 This project could take us into 2020 and ....
9 You have to send in your tax declaration .... 15 March at the latest.
10 I don't know what time she'll arrive; .... 3 o'clock I guess, or a bit later.

B Prepositions of time

Look at Mr Cottrell's diary and write sentences to describe the events. Today is 2 May.

EXAMPLE: *He's coming back from France at 4.45pm on 5 May.*

UNIT 14

Functions

ADVISING

1 *in my opinion, if I were you, it's worth* + verb + *-ing*, etc.

In my opinion, it would be better to take on temporary staff.

If I were you, I'd take the train; it's faster.

It's worth try**ing** to get an upgrade.

My advice would be to lobby the government.

In your shoes, I'd make a strong complaint.

Why not do some lateral thinking?

2 *'d better*

If you think you won't understand, you**'d better** use an interpreter.

In this case, *'d* is an abbreviation of *had* and not *would*. Note that the verb following *'d better* is used without *to*:

You**'d better** ask her for her permission before you go ahead. (NOT *to ask her)

He**'d better** not use the software without a site licence. (NOT *to use, *to not use)

3 Using the imperative

Be nice to her.

Remember to take your passport.

Think about it first.

Make sure you take enough money.

If the situation is dangerous, the advice is more like a warning:

Be careful.

Check your tyres before setting off on a long journey.

4 Using a negative form with *don't*

These statements offer advice in the form of a command:

Don't get discouraged.

Don't be afraid to take risks.

These statements function more as a warning:

Don't do anything without telling your boss first.

Don't buy shares in BKI – they're about to go into liquidation.

➡ *Giving instructions* page 128, for another use of the imperative

PRACTICE

A Giving advice

Complete the second sentence so that it has a similar meaning to the first one.

1 If you don't hurry, you'll miss the plane.
You'd ....

2 In my opinion, it would be better to sell your shares now.
My advice ....

3 It's not a good idea to drive through the city centre during rush hour.
Don't ....

4 Why don't you see a doctor if you're feeling ill?
You'd ....

5 I don't think it's advisable to tell her the bad news yet.
You'd ....

6 In my opinion, you ought to declare your overseas investments to the tax authorities.
If I ....

7 It's a good idea to ask for a second opinion.
It's worth ....

B If I were you, ...

You work for a firm of consultants that deals with HR and training issues. What would be your advice in the following situation?

Mr Mudd has been working in the same bank for 20 years and in Customer Relations for the past 15. He has had some temporary postings in other sections and once worked as a replacement in another branch. His job involves applying rules to routine cases and although his performance is competent and reliable, he is unwilling to take the initiative.

His work is basically that of a clerk but because of his length of service he earns quite a lot more than other, younger employees who do much the same kind of work. He recently turned down the opportunity to train to become a branch manager, saying, 'I'm happy in my job and I enjoy working in a team. I don't want to be in charge.'

AGREEING AND DISAGREEING

You can use the following words and expressions depending on the formality of the situation.

1 Agreeing

More formal	*Informal*
I completely / entirely / totally agree.	Right.
Yes, definitely.	Sure.
Yes, I'd go along with that.	Fine.
Yes, I agree with that wholeheartedly.	Great.
(NOT *I am agree with you.)	

2 Disagreeing

More formal	*Informal*
I don't agree.	Ridiculous.
(NOT *I am not agree.)	
I can't go along with that.	No way.
I disagree with that completely.	Over my dead body!
For me that is out of the question.	You're joking.

3 *So do I / Neither do I*, etc.

If you are in agreement with someone or have something in common, you can use *so* or *neither* to replace the noun phrase:

I'**m** very interested in archaeology.	So **am** I.
I **can't** stand waiting in airports.	Neither **can** I.
My wife and I **play** tennis a lot.	So **do** we.
I'**ll** be going to London soon.	So **will** I.
I **don't** believe politicians.	Neither **do** I.

4 Shades of opinion

You may have mixed feelings or not hold a strong opinion either way. In that case you can express a doubt or reservation:

I agree with you **to some extent** but ...

Yes, I'd go along with that **up to a point** but ...

That **may well be the case** although ...

You **may have a point** but ...

Yes, but **on the other hand** ...

Maybe, but we **still have to remember** that ...

Sometimes, especially in British English, these expressions are used to show politeness when you actually disagree but want to acknowledge the other speaker's contribution.

PRACTICE

A *so/neither*

Read the statements made by several speakers and agree with them, using *so* or *neither*.

EXAMPLE: 'I'm tired.' So am I.

1 'I didn't like *Jurassic Park*.' ....

2 'I can't stand people who are rude.' ....

3 'I should really exercise more.' ....

4 'I've never been to Fiji.' ....

5 'I enjoy going to the theatre.' ....

6 'I generally take a holiday in the summer.' ....

B Shades of opinion

How do you feel about the following? Write your ideas with a suitable expression of agreement or disagreement, as in the example.

	I agree entirely.	I agree to some extent.	I tend to disagree.	I completely disagree.
1 All men and women should do military service.				
2 There should be a single world currency.				
3 National industries should be protected.		Yes, I'd go along with that up to a point but you can't ignore market forces entirely.		
4 Bonuses are perfectly acceptable forms of remuneration.				
5 Men and women should retire at 55.				

ASKING FOR INFORMATION

1 Asking for a *Yes* or *No* response

All these questions use an *auxiliary* as the first word in the question and require a positive (*Yes*) or negative (*No*) answer:

Is Mohammed in his office?	Yes, he is.
Can you speak Arabic?	No, I can't.
Are you ready?	No, I'm not.
Do you belong to a union?	No, I don't.
Does your firm have a language policy?	No, it doesn't.
Has she finished the report?	Yes, she has.
Have the goods arrived at the frontier?	No, they haven't yet.
Should we have complained?	Yes, definitely.
Did they give a discount?	No, they didn't, actually.
Will they change the price?	No, they won't.

2 Open questions

We use this question form when we want more information than a simple confirmation or denial:

When will the order be sent?
Who is in charge of human resources?
Which is the best area to live in?
Whose car is blocking the entrance?
Where would you like to work?
What brand of washing powder do you use?
Why is he never on time?
How have you changed in the last five years?

The question word is placed before the auxiliary verb.

When we use a verb in a simple tense (present or past), we have to use the auxiliary *do / does / did* or a modal (*can / will / should*, etc.):

Where do you live?
Where can I get a taxi?
Why didn't they come?
Why couldn't she do it?
When does she want it?
When shall I arrive?
Where did you get it from?
Where would you like to go?
Who do you work with?
Who should I ask for?

3 Negative questions

We use a negative question when we suspect the answer will be *No*, having first thought it would be *Yes*:

Can't you get there earlier? (I think it's possible)
Won't 8 o'clock be too late? (I suspect it will be)
Didn't you tell them? (I thought you would)
Aren't you going? (I thought you were)

4 *Who*, *what* and *which*

When *who*, *what* or *which* is the *subject* of a sentence, an auxiliary is not used:

Who wants a lift to the station? (NOT *Who does want)
What happened at the meeting? (NOT *What did happen)
Which costs more? (NOT *Which does cost more?)

PRACTICE

A Asking questions

Fill in this questionnaire by writing the correct question forms.

Subject	*Question*	*Answer*
1 NAME	....What.... is your name?	Per Lysvag.
2 STATUS	.... you single or married?	I'm separated.
3 ADDRESS	.... do you live?	In Coventry.
4 AGE	.... are you?	27.
5 OCCUPATION	.... do you do for a living?	I'm an engineer.
6 LENGTH OF SERVICE	.... have you been working for your present employer?	Three years.
7 SALARY	.... do you earn?	£50,000 a year.
8 FOREIGN TRAVEL	.... do you go abroad?	Three or four times a year, mostly back to Sweden.
9 ENGLISH AT WORK	.... did you last have to make a presentation in English?	Last week at a meeting in Birmingham.
10 REASON FOR LANGUAGE TRAINING	.... do you need training in foreign languages?	To speak with my colleagues and customers abroad.
11 LANGUAGE ABILITY	.... of these words describes your ability in English: beginner, intermediate or advanced?	Advanced, I hope!

B A bad line

Sue Watson is phoning Bill Daniels about a recent open day, but her mobile phone battery is low and sometimes she can't be heard. Write the questions Bill has to ask.

Sue It was a great success. More than **xxxxx** people visited the plant.

Bill Sorry. ....[1] the plant?

Sue Over 2,000. And **xxxxx** congratulated you on your excellent organisation!

Bill I can't hear you. ....[2] me?

Sue The **xxxxx** director complimented you on your organisation.

Bill Sorry? ....[3] complimented me?

Sue The divisional director. Look, it's a really bad line. I'll talk to you later.

COMPARING PRODUCTS AND SERVICES

There are many ways of making a comparison between one thing and another.

1 Short adjectives

The cost of living is **higher** in Tokyo **than** in Bucharest.

A CD or a mobile phone bought in France is **cheaper than** (one bought) in the UK.

2 Short adjectives ending in *-y*

Learning Chinese was **easier than** I thought.

British families are **healthier than** they were two decades ago but are no **happier**, according to an official survey.

3 Longer adjectives

Mobile phone accessories are **more profitable than** the phone itself.

Solar power can be **less expensive than** other sources of energy.

4 *more* + noun + *than*

She earns **more** money **than** I do.

We made **more** profit **than** we did last year.

It is often possible to use *more / less than* without a noun:

He knows **more than** he says he does. Pay **less than** $100 a year and benefit from our special offer.

5 Superlatives

Short adjectives: Burj Dubai is **the highest** building in the world.

Long adjectives: Moscow is **the most expensive** city in the world.

6 *as ... as*

There were not **as many** layoffs **as** we originally anticipated.
In 2009 one euro was worth **about as much as** one UK pound.
Instruction manuals for TV sets in Europe cost **as much as** the glass in the screen.

7 Ranking

A bottle of Chanel No. 5 costs **a third more** in the UK **than** in France.

Ski boots are **27% more expensive** in the US **than** in Sweden.

Distribution and marketing costs are **much higher** in Europe **than** in the US.

8 Other ways of comparing

Fourth-quarter sales were up 14% **compared with / to** the previous year.

The imported model is 30% cheaper and **compares** favourably in quality.

By / In comparison with other European countries, car prices in the UK are very high.

PRACTICE

A Making comparisons

Match the ways in which comparisons can be made 1–8 with the examples a–h.

1 comparative adjective + *than*
2 *more* / *less* + comparative adjective + *than*
3 *more* + noun + *than*
4 *as* + quantifier + *as*
5 *a* + comparative adjective + noun
6 numeral + *more than*
7 quantifier + comparative adjective + *than*
8 a superlative

a) as much as
b) cheaper than in the UK
c) the highest / the most expensive
d) less expensive than
e) much higher than
f) more profit than
g) a bigger country
h) £77 more than

B Common mistakes

Correct the errors in these sentences.

1 Lisbon is not as big than London.
2 There is more to life that a spreadsheet.
3 The disadvantage of this project is that it is not as cheap than the other.
4 Women's pay is more lower than men's, even for the same work.
5 Metro is the world's second bigger retailer after Wal-Mart Stores of the US.

C Global MBA rankings

Look at the table and complete the following paragraph with these expressions.

more or less the same | more than | much faster | much more | closest | compared with | the highest | the most significant

FT

Name of business school	Country	Average salary 3 years after graduation ($)	Salary percentage increase after graduation	Career progress rank/100	Value for money rank/100
University of Pennsylvania: Wharton	USA	169,784	119	69	100
London Business School	UK	146,565	121	22	56
Harvard Business School	USA	163,637	115	41	86
Columbia Business School	USA	164,310	132	33	81
Insead	France/Singapore	147,908	108	23	7
Stanford Graduate School of Business	USA	170,340	105	13	94

Among the six top business schools worldwide, graduates achieve ....[1] salaries in the USA. ....[2] salary increase is for graduates from Columbia, ...[3] ten percentage points higher than its ....[4] rival. However, ...[5] American and British schools, Insead gives ....[6] value for money. Career progess measured in terms of promotion and seniority is ....[7] at Stanford than at the others. The next best are the London Business School and Insead, where the rate of progress is ....[8].

COMPLAINING AND APOLOGISING

1 Complaining to someone you know well

If we are annoyed at someone's behaviour, we can say:

I'm fed up with your attitude.

I've had enough of it.

I wish you wouldn't ...

I'd rather you didn't ...

If the complaint mentions the person concerned, we use a pronoun + verb + *-ing*:

I'm fed up with his tell**ing** me what to do all the time.

I'm sick (**to death**) **of their** complain**ing**.

We can also use *always* + the present continuous to express annoyance:

You**'re always** try**ing** to control what I do.

You**'re** always mak**ing** such a fuss.

2 Complaining in a public place

If we have already complained and nothing has been done, then we can say:

I want to see the manager / person in charge.

I'm afraid I'm not satisfied with the standard of service.

I'd like to make a (**formal**) **complaint** about the hygiene.

3 Complaining in writing

We can start the letter in a number of ways:

I regret to have to complain about ...

I am writing to complain about ...

I am writing to express my concern about ...

I would like to make a complaint about ...

4 Threatening

In order to back up a complaint, we can promise to do something unpleasant if we do not receive satisfaction. We can make a threat by using *if* or *unless*:

Unless I receive compensation, I will have to take legal action.
I would be reluctant to change suppliers, but **if** the situation does not improve, I will be forced to look elsewhere.

➡ *Conditionals* page 34

5 Apologising

In speech it is common to say *I'm sorry / I'm extremely sorry for (the delay).*
In writing, the following are common:

We (sincerely) apologise for the misunderstanding.
I assure you we are doing everything in our power to put things right.
I fully appreciate your position and very much regret the inconvenience this has caused.

PRACTICE

A A letter of complaint

The sentences in this letter of complaint are in the wrong order. Rewrite them in the correct order and insert these words and expressions.

I am writing to express my concern	Regrettably,	I will have no alternative but to

Dear Mrs O'Malley,

However, if the delay continues, ... [1] give instructions to suspend payment of your last invoice.

.... [2] about the failure to supply the essential components which were promised us for 1 April and which do not seem to have reached us.

Given the long-standing relationship between our two firms, I would be reluctant to change suppliers.

I look forward to your response.

.... [3] this delay is now causing a bottleneck in our production.

Yours sincerely,

B A letter of apology

Complete Mrs O'Malley's reply with these phrases.

We very much regret	Once again, we apologise	We are very concerned
hope you will understand the reason	I assure you we are doing everything in our power	

.... [1] to hear that the consignment of spare parts that was ordered from us in February has not reached you. .... [2] the disruption this has caused to your production.

.... [3] to make sure the consignment arrives as soon as possible. The delay is owing to an expected delivery of components from Spain which has been held up as a result of industrial unrest. However, the components have now arrived and the consignment has been sent to you air freight.

.... [4] for the inconvenience and .... [5].

CONFIRMING INFORMATION

Question tags are used when we expect the person we are speaking with to agree with us or to confirm that what we are saying is right. They are most often used in spoken English.

FORM Tags are formed using an auxiliary and the pronoun referring to the subject. The tag is almost always contracted.

Affirmative main clause	*Negative tag*
It**'s** hot today,	**isn't** it?
You **were** there,	**weren't** you?
You**'re** Canadian,	**aren't** you?
She **can** drive,	**can't** she?
You **will** stay in touch,	**won't** you?

Negative main clause	*Positive tag*
The meeting **isn't** today,	**is** it?
She **wasn't** present,	**was** she?
They**'re not** coming,	**are** they?
She **shouldn't** know,	**should** she?
She **couldn't** get there,	**could** she?

If the main clause does not have an auxiliary or the verb *to be*, we use *do*, *does* or *did* in the tag:

You **agree** with me, **don't** you?

You **don't like** raw fish, **do** you?

She **gave** you her number, **didn't** she?

He **doesn't drink** alcohol, **does** he?

When *have* is used for states (e.g. possession), both *do* and *have* are used for the tag in British English but *do* is normal in American English:

You have a motorbike, **don't** you / **haven't** you?

Your father has a yacht, **doesn't** he / **hasn't** he?

The tag for *I am* is *aren't I?*

I**'m** not late, **am** I? I**'m** late, **aren't** I?

USES 1 Asking a real question

If we really want an answer to the question, the voice goes up at the end of the question:

The meeting's at 10 o'clock, isn't it? ↗

You do agree, don't you? ↗

2 Asking for agreement

If the question is not a real one, we use falling intonation:

It's a nice day, isn't it? ↘

You have to wait a long time, don't you? ↘

3 Making offers or suggestions

I**'ll** get you a drink, **shall I**?

Let's pencil in Thursday, **shall we**?

PRACTICE

A Confirming decisions

The people taking part in the conversation below are trying to remember what was said during a recent meeting. Complete the conversation with appropriate question tags.

A What did we say Janice was going to do?

B Janice was going to revise the estimates, ... [1]?

C I think so. And she said she would talk to Aziz about it, ... [2]?

A Are you sure?

B Perhaps. But Bill wanted to change the procedure, ... [3]?

C He didn't say that, ... [4]?

B I thought he did. But it wouldn't work, ... [5]? We agreed on that, ... [6]?

A I can't remember to be honest. We should have taken notes, ... [7]?

B Yes, it's terrible, ... [8]? We'd better have the meeting again, ... [9]?

A OK, let's make it first thing Monday morning, ... [10]?

C OK by me.

B A conversation at a cocktail party

Complete the conversation, which takes place at a cocktail reception held at an embassy.

A Hello, you're Mick Harvey, ... [1]?

B That's right. How do you know my name?

A You were the commercial attaché in Egypt.

B That's right. Oh yes, and you were working for Amoco, ... [2]?

A Yes, but I left six months ago.

B The weather's wonderful, ... [3]?

A Too hot for me. Is that the ambassador over there?

B Yes. You've met him, ... [4]?

A No, actually I haven't.

B Well, I'll introduce you, ... [5]?

DESCRIBING A COMPANY

Read this description of Nestlé and note how the information is organised:

Nestlé, whose head office is in Vevey on the shores of Lake Geneva, is the world's largest food company. Although we are Switzerland's biggest industrial enterprise, only two per cent of sales are generated in Switzerland.
We are a global company employing 276,000 people on every continent. Consequently, our management and staff reflect a truly international outlook.

Nestlé now produces the world's favorite brands in 480 factories worldwide. In 140 years of growth and diversification, we have never lost sight of our core business: improving the quality of people's lives through high-quality, nutritious and convenient prepared foods and beverages. Today, Nestlé brands are present on almost every supermarket shelf, and some products – like Nescafé, Findus, Perrier and Maggi – are sold in more than 100 countries.

Geography:	multinational, head office in Switzerland
Employees:	276,000 people on five continents
Activity:	the world's largest food company, producing global brands
Production facilities:	480 factories worldwide
Financial information:	market capitalisation 195 billion Swiss francs

Other useful phrases include:

Geography:	We are based in / located in / situated in ...
Employees:	We employ *n* people / there are *n* people on the payroll
Activity:	Our firm specialises in / produces / manufactures / supplies ...
Type:	a joint venture
	a subsidiary
	a holding company
Position:	is the leading company in its field
	ranks number one in the market for ...
	is a major player / operates in many different markets
	is a group ranking among the world's top 20 ....
	recently established
	well-established
	with a long tradition of success
Financial information:	achieving annual turnover of $*n*
	generating profits of ....

PRACTICE

A HMV

Complete the extract with these words.

operates | worldwide | the world's foremost | consists of | leading

HMV Media Group plc .... [1] HMV, one of .... [2] specialist music retailers, and Waterstones and Dillons, the two .... [3] brands in the UK book retailing market. The group .... [4] in many different markets with nearly 700 stores .... [5], generating sales of almost £2 billion.

B Wieden+Kennedy

Complete the extract with these words.

headquarters | range | world-class | employs | headquartered | located | operations

Wieden+Kennedy is a .... [1] advertising agency, ... [2] in the USA with .... [3] all over the globe. Its clients........................ [4] from Coca-Cola to Microsoft and Nike. Wieden+Kennedy's European........................ [5] is .... [6] in Amsterdam and........................ [7] approximately 120 people.

C Sita

Using the information in the box, write a description of Sita as the first paragraph for the job advertisement below.

Geography:	Geneva-based, present in 220 countries (900+ locations)
Staff:	3,400
Activity:	telecommunications (more than 1,800 customers, 24/7)
Position:	largest communications network
Revenues:	$1.42bn

INTERNATIONAL TAX MANAGER FT

....

....

....

- SITA provides a one-stop shop for all mission-critical business-to-business communications and information needs
- Our client is seeking to recruit a tax specialist who has a strong track record in practice and/or commerce/industry.

DESCRIBING PROCESSES

Focusing on information

When describing a process, we focus more on what is done than on who does it. For this reason, the passive is commonly used, as in the passage below on recycling paper.

Recycling Paper

First, the paper **is sorted** by type or grade. Then the separated paper **is put** into a large vat (similar to a giant kitchen mixer) and **mixed** with water, creating a product called 'slurry'. The slurry **is pumped** onto a moving wire screen and most of the water **is extracted**. The resulting paper sheet, or web, **is squeezed** between large rollers to remove most of the water. The semi-dry web is then run through heated dryer rollers to eliminate the remaining water. Each stage of the process **has to be monitored** by state-of-the-art control equipment.

When dry, the paper **is wound** onto rollers for storage and then later **cut up** into whatever size **will be needed** for the new product.

Unlike glass or steel, paper degrades each time it **is recycled**. However, when wood or cotton fibres are added, the slurry **can be turned into** office-grade paper.

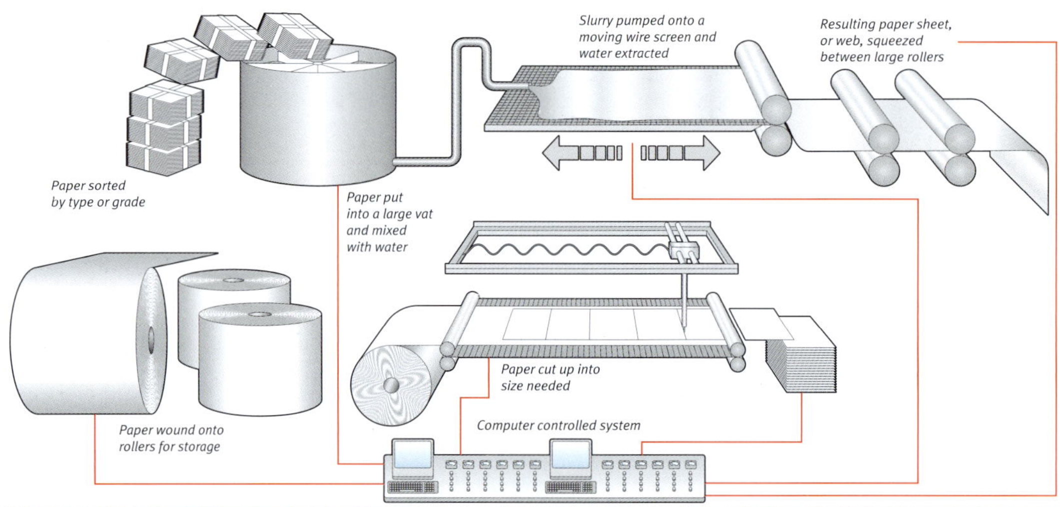

Mixing active and passive verb forms

It is also possible to mention what actions people or things perform in a process as well as focusing on the action itself. So there is a mixture of active and passive.

Creating a news story

Whenever a disaster happens somewhere in the world, reporters and photographers are sent there to interview people and take pictures. The news reports and photos are sent by e-mail or by special satellite link.
Then other journalists edit the stories and select the pictures. Designers work on the stories and photos on-screen in order to get the layout right. The final text and photo files are then sent to a plate-making machine. A thin metal plate is made for each page of the newspaper, wrapped around a roller on the printing press and coated with ink. When all the pages have been printed, they are put together in the right order. The finished newspapers are finally tied into bundles and delivered to newsstands.

➡ *Passives* (2) page 50

PRACTICE

A Active or passive?

Complete the passage with either active or passive forms of the verbs.

Manufacturing resource planning – MRP – is a process which ....[1] (integrate) marketing, production and sales. MRP ....[2] (rely) upon a fully integrated process and ....[3] (coordinate) by a master scheduler, who ....[4] (ensure) that each of the three phases ....[5] (manage) cost-effectively and efficiently.

In MRP, all the projections, estimates and forecasts have to ....[6] (synthesise) in a production plan into concrete stages and mixes of products, whose manufacture has to ....[7] (schedule) as cost-effectively as possible, using just-in-time and electronic data interchange systems. Each stage in the production process ....[8] (give) a separate coding.

Thus all arriving raw materials or bought-in parts ....[9] (check) for quality and will not ....[10] (use) until set standards have ....[11] (meet). Similarly, finished goods may not ....[12] (warehouse) until quality checks have ....[13] (fulfil). At each stage all materials and items ....[14] (give) unique production batch codings for identification in case of a defect occurring.

In this way a computer database ....[15] (build up) of each and every production run. In the case of a product recall, any defect problems may ....[16] (locate) quickly and the public relations damage will therefore ....[17] (limit).

From *Business: A Student's Guide*

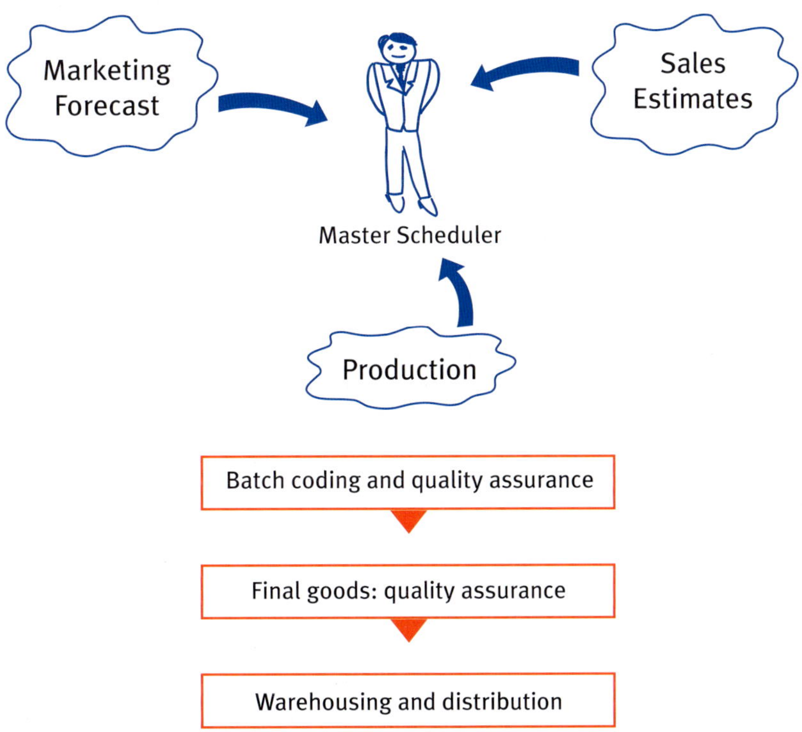

DESCRIBING TRENDS

1 Present trends

When we describe a trend, we describe a changing, developing situation. Therefore, to describe ongoing trends we use either the *present continuous* (➡ page 10) or the *present perfect continuous* (➡ page 26):

In Britain, people **are living** longer.

The number of single-parent families **is increasing**.

The British **are eating** more and more convenience foods and drinking more wine than ever before.

The proportion of a family's income spent on entertainment **has been rising**.

2 Trends that began in the past and have reached an end-point

We use the present perfect when a trend has come to completion:

The re-engineering of our firm **has created** a flatter hierarchy.

The European consumer **has become** more sophisticated.

3 How long?

If we want to say how long a trend has lasted, we can use a number of time expressions.

We use *during* or *in*, *from* and *until* with periods in the past:

During the first few years we were just breaking even.

The world slumped into depression **in** the 1930s.

From the mid-1980s government spending tended to go down.

Things were going well **until** the stock market crash.

Time up to the present can be expressed using *for*, *since* and *over*:

We've been targeting a different market segment **for** the last two years. (*for* + duration)

They've been heading for a fall **since** last February. (*since* + point in time)

We've increased our market share **over** the last five years. (from five years ago up to now)

PRACTICE

A

Trends in consumer relationships

Read the extract and decide whether the trends described have reached an end-point or are still developing. Then choose a suitable form for the verbs in brackets. There may be more than one possible answer.

In the days before mass marketing, the local bank manager knew the names and ages of his customers' children, the corner shop knew which brand of breakfast cereal to stock for local families and businessmen bought their suits tailor-made.

But all that ....[1] (change). Today, under the onslaught of cost-cutting, rationalisation and automation, many people ....[2] (never see) their bank manager, an impersonal supermarket checkout ....[3] (replace) the cosy corner shop and most people ....[4] (never have) a suit made to measure.

Further radical change is under way. More and more companies ....[5] (realise) that the conventional mass-production model on which consumer marketing ....[6] (be) based no longer works.

Instead of focusing narrowly on cost-cutting measures and improving efficiency, more and more market leaders ....[7] (re-examine) their business strategies and deciding that customer services and customer relationship management are the keys to future growth.

Increasingly, companies ....[8] (take) a holistic view of their customer relationships and focusing on the lifetime value of those relationships. It costs five to eight times more to acquire a customer than it does to retain an existing one. Consequently, customer relationship management – CRM for short – ....[9] (become) one of the hottest new fields of consultancy.

FT

B

Describing trends

Write sentences describing the trends in the graphs below. Use one or more of the time expressions on the previous page.

Trends in overall online travel market size – Europe 1998–2007 ..2009

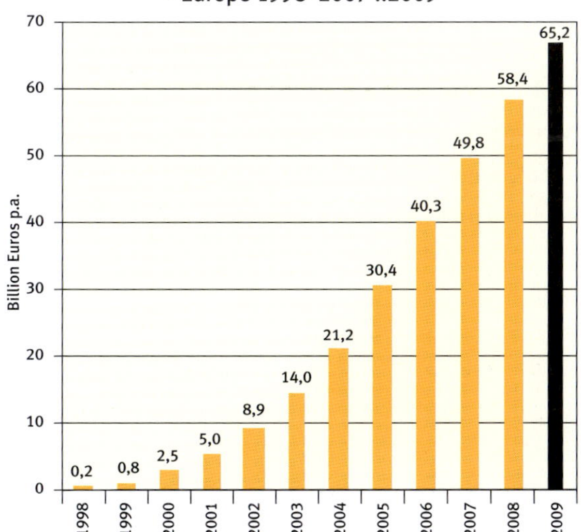

Retail sales trends

Source: Carl H. Marcussen. Centre for Regional and Tourism Research. www.crt.dk/trends. 23 March 2009.

FORECASTING AND SPECULATING

1 Forecasting

We use *will* to make predictions about the future:

In the future everybody **will** be famous for fifteen minutes. (Andy Warhol)

A spacecraft **will** land on Mars in the next twenty years or so.

We use *likely to* if we think something is probably going to happen and *bound to* if we are 100% certain:

My memory's getting worse so I'm **likely to** forget.

He hasn't done any work at all. He's **bound to** fail his examination.

→ *The future* page 28

2 Speculating

We use *if* + past simple + conditional to make a hypothesis about the future:

If I **knew** how the stock markets were going to react, I **would** get rich.

If work **was** (or **were**) such a splendid thing, the rich **would** keep more of it for themselves.

We use modal verbs to make deductions about present situations:

He left an hour ago and it's not far so he **will** / **must** be there by now. (100% certain)

He left 45 minutes ago and it's not far so he **should** be there by now. (reasonably certain)

He left 30 minutes ago and it's not far so he **may** / **might** be there by now. (possible but uncertain)

He only left 15 minutes ago and it's quite far so he **can't** / **won't** be there yet. (impossible)

→ *Modal verbs* page 52

3 Speculating about the past

We use *if* + past perfect + conditional to make a hypothesis about the past:

If he **had got** better grades at school, he **would have gone** to university.

If I **hadn't been** in the right place at the right time, I **wouldn't have got** the opportunity.

Must and *can't* are also used to make suppositions about the past:

The door was locked so the thieves **must have got in** through the window.

I wasn't there myself but the atmosphere **must have been** electric.

He says he met me in Brussels but he **can't have** – I've never been there.

She looked so surprised when I arrived, she **can't have been expecting** me.

→ *Conditionals* page 34

PRACTICE

A Forecasting

What is in store for you, your company and your country? Write sentences using *bound to*, *likely to* or *unlikely to* about the following.

1 a pay rise
2 a takeover
3 redundancy
4 promotion
5 a change of government in the next six months

B Speculating

Match the sentence halves and complete the blanks with *must* or *can't*.

1 She looks so young;
2 She can speak English and Spanish perfectly;
3 She .... know what's in the report;
4 She .... have friends in high places
5 She .... know Berlin pretty well;
6 She .... have much of a social life;

a) she .... come from a bilingual family.
b) she ......can't...... be a day over 30.
c) she works 60 hours a week.
d) she lived there for three years.
e) she hasn't had a copy.
f) because she's survived three major scandals.

C Making hypotheses

What can you infer about these situations?

1 The director suddenly bought a huge block of shares when everybody else was selling theirs. Then the share price soared by 25%.
2 The fish in the canteen smelt strange yesterday and subsequently a number of employees have not reported for work.
3 She insists that he spoke to her in Urdu but he's never learnt a word of Urdu in his life.
4 There is an unexplained loss of £1.5 million in the company accounts and the finance director has been absent from work for the last eight days.

GETTING THINGS DONE

1 If we arrange for something to be done by someone else, we say that we *get* or *have* it done for us. *Have* is slightly more formal:

Subject	*get / have*	*Object*	*Past participle*
We	**are getting**	our offices	**redecorated**.
Could you	**have**	this payment	**authorised** by the accounts department?
They	**get**	their catalogue	**printed** in Mexico.
We've always	**had**	the machines	**assembled** on another site.

2 We can use *have* followed by an object + base form of the verb if we want to emphasise who does or did the work we arranged:

I always **have** my secretary **check** my spelling.

I **had** the maintenance people **test** the air conditioning.

She **had** the catering staff **prepare** a meal for the guests.

If we want to use *get* we use an object + *to*-infinitive:

I always **get** my secretary **to check** my spelling.

I **got** the maintenance people **to test** the air conditioning.

She **got** the catering staff **to prepare** a meal for the guests.

3 There are a number of verbs that describe action undertaken to make sure something is done:

attend to   contend with   cope with   deal with   follow up (on)   handle   process
see to   tackle   take care of

Mrs Baker **deals with** all requests for product information.

It's my job to **see to** all routine maintenance work.

There are a lot of things to **attend to** before the trade fair.

You should allow three working days for your order to be **processed**.

It is our policy to **follow up on** all customer complaints.

Her assistant is ill and I don't know how she is **coping with** the extra workload.

PRACTICE

A Getting things done

Rewrite the sentences using *have* or *get*. Decide whether or not you want to emphasise who does or did the work.

1 All our export risks are insured.

We ....

2 The garage services my car every 15,000 kilometres.

I ....

3 A specialist agency translates all the company documentation and manuals. (two possible answers)

We ....

We ....

4 We've asked the contractors to build a new extension. (two possible answers)

We're ....

We're ....

5 The legal department drew up the contract on my instructions. (two possible answers)

I ....

I ....

B Arranging for things to be done

React to the statements below using the verbs in brackets, as in the example.

EXAMPLE:

My passport expires soon. (renew)

I need to have it renewed.

1 The printer only works sporadically. (fix)

....

2 Mrs Baxter is going on a training course. (replace)

....

3 The outside windows are incredibly dirty. (clean)

....

4 I'm not sure the figures are entirely accurate. (check)

....

GIVING INSTRUCTIONS

1 Using the imperative

We use the base form of the verb to give instructions and issue warnings, as in the following extract from a technical manual.

- **Turn** the pump pressure off at the control panel.
- **Hold** the gun over an appropriate empty container and **lock** the gun in an open position.
- **Remove** the injector.
- **Disconnect** the air supply from the system.

DANGER:
Do not attempt to remove, repair or clean an accumulator until you have relieved pressure.

- Using your hand, **unscrew** the filter tank from the filter body. (see figure 66).

  ⚠ **Do not use** a wrench.
- **Remove** the filter core and the screen from the filter tank (see figure 67).
- **Inspect** the filter core and screen, then **clean** with solvent.

2 Using the present simple

The following instructions mix the imperative and the present simple:

This is how you get to our office from the train station. Turn left as you come out and walk down Richmond Street. You continue for about 100 metres and turn right at the bank. You then cross over the canal and you will see a high-rise office building in front of you. We are on the seventh floor.

3 Giving special instructions

You can stress the importance of your instructions by prefacing them with a number of phrases:

Make sure you wear appropriate protective clothing.

Do not forget to turn off the electricity supply before opening the panel.

Always use the correct lubricating fluid.

Never clean your clothing with compressed air.

PRACTICE

A Changing a wheel

Match the pictures to the instructions and put them in the correct order.

- [ ] Prise out the centre hub cap.
- [ ] Lower the vehicle and remove the jack.
- [ ] Replace the centre hub cap.
- [ ] Unscrew the wheel bolts.
- [1] Park the car on a flat, stable surface and apply the handbrake firmly. C
- [ ] Remove the wheel and replace it with the spare.
- [ ] Raise the vehicle off the ground with a jack.
- [ ] Tighten the wheel bolts.

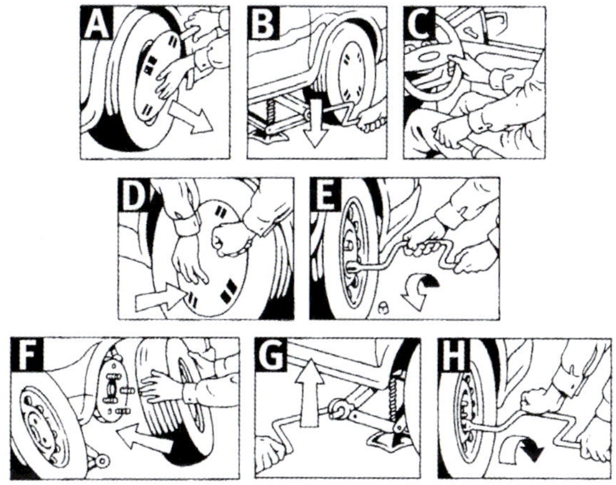

B Giving directions

Debbie Scott works as a secretary. Her new divisional manager has to go to the London headquarters next week to attend a meeting and he has decided to drive there.

Debbie is ringing another secretary, Judith, to get exact directions. Trace the route on the map and mark where the headquarters are located.

Judith I think his best bet is to follow the signs to Central London and the City and cross the Thames at Tower Bridge.

Debbie ... signs to Central London and the City and cross the Thames at Tower Bridge.

Judith That's right. Cross that, the World Trade Centre is on your right and the Tower of London on the left and then, um, take the second right. There's a one-way system and then take the first left at the roundabout into Mansell Street and then left again into Aldgate High Street.

Debbie ... into Old Gate High Street.

Judith No, Aldgate: A-L-D-G-A-T-E High Street. And then after the tube station, right and right again into **xxxxx** Street and we're just on the left. There's an underground car park so there's no problem with parking.

Debbie Sorry, what was the name of the street again?

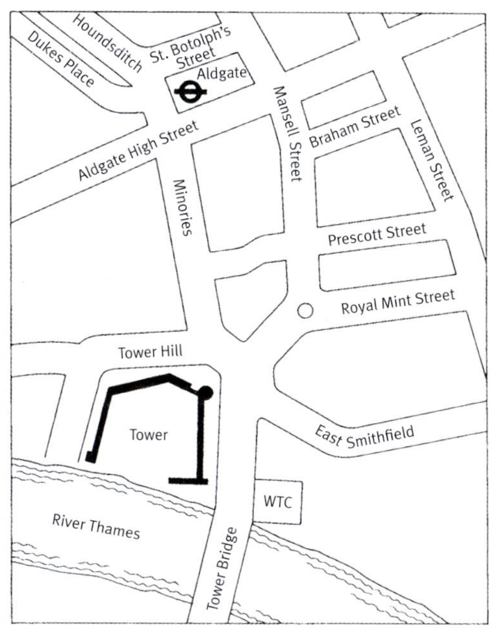

PLANNING AHEAD

1 Making plans

We most often use the present continuous for plans made before the time of speaking:

I'm meeting Carlos for dinner tomorrow evening.

Next week **I'm visiting** a supplier in Warsaw.

It is also possible to use the verbs *plan* and *intend* in either the present simple or present continuous:

I **plan to** / **am planning to** have everything ready by June.

She **intends to** / **is intending to** return to work after she's had the baby.

➡ *Present continuous* page 12

2 Making arrangements

To speak about a definite arrangement for the future we can use *be going to* + verb:

I'm going to go freelance shortly.

We**'re going to** talk about staffing levels at the next opportunity.

➡ *The future* page 28

3 Talking about unfulfilled plans

We use *mean to* or *want to* when we have forgotten to do something we were planning to do or we have not had the chance to do it yet:

I've been meaning to get in touch with Katya but I haven't got round to it.

I know he**'s been wanting to** talk to you about it.

4 Setting out to do something

We use the expression *to set out to do something* when we decide to do something and make plans for it to be achieved:

We **set out** to be the number one player in the industry.

She **set out** with the intention of becoming chief executive.

5 Describing arrangements

We can use the future continuous to describe the plans and arrangements we have made:

I'm in Munich next week and I**'ll be seeing** Herr Röstel then.

When you're in London next month, you**'ll be staying** at the Birkbeck Hotel.

For plans completed before a deadline we use the future perfect:

By this time next year we**'ll have completed** the reorganisation.

➡ *The future* page 28

PRACTICE

A Making arrangements

A London-based consultancy called MarkUp is planning a seminar called *The Effective Global Manager*. The seminar organiser has received a copy of the provisional programme drawn up by a colleague who has made notes. Expand these notes into full questions.

Location	Grosvenor House Hotel, Park Lane
Date	Monday–Wednesday (18–20) March
Provisional programme	Which printer? No. of copies? [1]
Sunday 17 March	
Delegates arrive at City Airport	Transport? [2]
	Evening entertainment? [3]
Monday 18 March	
Opening address	Who? [4]
The changing business environment	Simon Kelly
Lunch	
Cross-cultural communication	Pieter Oet
Communicating assertively	Dwight Wayne
Cocktail and dinner	And then? [5]
Tuesday 19 March	
Plenary session	Rod Weir Which room? [6]
	What subject? [7]
Re-engineering the corporation	Philip Price
Lunch	What about vegetarians? [8]
The learning manager	Gavin Tudor
Workshops	various – How many rooms? [9]
	What size? [10] Equipment? [11]
Wednesday 20 March	
Strategies, staff and systems	Lara Ford
Lunch	
Financial skills	Michael Reynolds
Transfer to airport	Time? [12]

EXAMPLE: Who is going to print the programme? How many copies will you be needing?

....

....

REPORTING WHAT PEOPLE SAY OR THINK (1)

FORM When reporting speech we can either use direct speech or indirect speech:

1 Using direct speech

We use the same words as the original speaker or reformulate them:

Actual words: 'We are not going to compromise with terrorists.'

Report: So then the minister said, 'We are not going to compromise with terrorists.'

2 Using indirect speech

We make the speaker's words part of our sentence, changing verb forms and pronouns as necessary. It is not necessary to follow *said* by *that*:

The minister said (that) they were not going to compromise with terrorists.

3 Reporting things just said

'Oh hello, Janet, Charles has just phoned and he **says** he **wants** to see you.'

The situation is still present.

4 Reporting things said in the past

We normally put the tense of the verbs originally used one tense back in the past if the original words were said some time ago:

Original verb	*Reported verb*
'I **don't** know how to cook an omelette.'	He said he **didn't** know how to cook an omelette.
'She **is** getting annoyed.'	He said that she **was** getting annoyed.
'I**'ve** forgotten the code.'	He said he **had** forgotten the code.
'I**'ve been** trying to get through.'	She said she **had been** trying to get through.
'They **will** never agree.'	She said they **would** never agree.

If the original verb is already in the past tense, it is not necessary to use the past perfect:

'Martin **sent** them the invoice.'	She said that Martin (**had**) **sent** them the invoice.

5 Using modal verbs

Modal verbs do not change:

'You **could** / **might** / **should** go.'	She said that we **could** / **might** / **should** go.
'I **would** like to leave.'	He said he **would** like to leave.

PRACTICE

A Reporting what the MD said

These are some of the things that the managing director said at a meeting you attended recently. A colleague who was unable to attend wants you to tell her what the MD said.

1 'I think a joint venture is the best way to break into the Middle East.'

....

2 'We are not planning to set up a subsidiary.'

....

3 'We've been talking to a group of investors in the Gulf.'

....

4 'I've talked to the commercial attaché at the embassy.'

....

5 'I don't want to diversify in the immediate future.'

....

6 'We shouldn't attempt to move too fast because we might get our fingers burnt.'

....

7 'We will be sending Stuart Campbell on a fact-finding mission.'

....

B News in brief

Match the sentence halves.

A

1 Richard Pound, the International Olympic Committee official leading the investigation into the corruption scandal engulfing the Olympic movement, said yesterday
2 The director of the Office of Fair Trading said that car manufacturers
3 The catering industry said that the new rules on genetically modified food
4 The European Union's trade commissioner said that
5 Britain and the US have told the United Nations

B

a) would be unenforceable and would put an unacceptable burden on food outlets.
b) the EU was prepared to put all its tariffs on the table for negotiation in the next round of talks.
c) were using recommended resale prices to mask the true selling price of vehicles.
d) to exclude their citizens from UN staff beginning to return to Afghanistan.
e) the IOC had been trying 'for years' to find proof that its members took bribes from bidding cities.

REPORTING WHAT PEOPLE SAY OR THINK (2)

1 Informing

Would you like to **tell** her that she is being made redundant?

NL Industries **said** it **intended** to cut debt and increase capacity.

Indonesian police **told** reporters they were questioning three former central bank directors.

Note that *tell* and *told* are followed by a person object (*tell her*, *told reporters*, etc.).

2 Instructing

I don't like autocratic bosses who **tell** employees **to work** harder.

She **told** him **to improve** his performance.

The court **told** the firm **to pay** £750,000 in compensation.

When *tell* and *told* are used in this way, they are followed by a person object + infinitive.

3 Reporting the speaker's attitude and intention

Note how the reporting verbs are used in the following extract:

The president **acknowledged** last week that the economy was in recession, commonly defined as two consecutive quarters of negative growth. The Economy Minister's office also **admitted** in a statement that the risk of contraction for a second quarter between July and September was now 'real'. However, the president **insisted** that corrective action was being taken and **warned** opposition leaders against making political capital out of a situation that required national unity.

4 Some reporting verbs are followed by a person object + infinitive

'If I were you, I'd keep quiet.'	She **advised her colleague** to keep quiet.
'Don't sell your shares yet.'	He **warned me** not to sell my shares yet.
'Don't forget to take your passport.'	He **reminded her** to take her passport.

Others are followed by an infinitive:

'I'll send you a cheque.'	He **promised** to send her a cheque.
'We'll sue you if you cancel.'	They **threatened** to sue us if we cancelled.
'I'll give you a lift if you like.'	She **offered** to give me a lift.

Note that *suggest* and *recommend* are followed by two possible structures:

'You could hire more temporary staff.' She **suggested** hir**ing** more temporary staff.

She **suggested that** he **hire** more temporary staff.

PRACTICE

A The minutes of a meeting

Read this transcript from a meeting. Then complete the extract below with the reporting verbs from the box which most accurately reflect what each speaker said.

Robert Dunne	Right, let's start. The main item on the agenda is whether we reorganise our operations in France. I'd like to hear your views about this. Can you put us in the picture, John?
John Marsh	Yes. As you all know, we set up a regional centre in Lille two years ago. We hoped it would be a base for expansion into other areas of France and Benelux. Unfortunately, I have to say that it hasn't been a success. It hasn't made the kind of impact we expected and, as I see it, it's going to be very difficult to get much of a return on our investment.
Robert Dunne	Thank you, John. How do you feel about this, Gillian?
Gillian Hall	Well, if you remember, I told everybody at the time that I was not in favour of Lille as a location. We should never have set up there. If you want to gain a foothold in the French market, you've got to be in the capital.
Robert Dunne	Thank you, Gillian. What's your reaction, Mark? Do you think Gillian's right?
Mark Atkins	No, I don't agree at all. Benelux is a big market and Lille is right from a geographical point of view. I really think we need to give them more time.
Gillian Hall	Well, you've got a point, but what about the rest of France? You've got to be in Paris, like I said.
Penny Mure	I think the local staff is useless. They haven't done what they're employed to do. They never reply when I try to get in touch with them.
Robert Dunne	Is that true?
Gillian Hall	Yeah, that's happened to me on several occasions.
John Marsh	Look. Why don't we bring in a French consultancy to analyse the situation for us? We obviously need more information about what is going on.
Robert Dunne	OK, I'll look for a suitable firm of consultants in the next few days. If we don't do something quickly, we'll just lose out to our competitors.

invited	pointed out	confirmed	disagreed	raised	reminded	advised
warned	complained	outlined	suggested	offered	acknowledged	

Mr Dunne .... [1] the issue of operations in France and the siting of the regional centre in Lille and .... [2] comments from the review committee. Mr Marsh .... [3] the reasons for choosing Lille and .... [4] that it had not been a success. Ms Hall .... [5] the meeting that she had never been in favour of Lille and .... [6] that it was important to have a presence in Paris in order to gain a foothold in France. Mr Atkins .... [7] and .... [8] the committee to allow the Lille centre to continue for the time being. Ms Mure .... [9] and Ms Hall .... [10] that the staff in Lille were apparently incompetent. Mr Marsh .... [11] that they hire a consultancy to investigate. Mr Dunne .... [12] to look for a suitable firm and .... [13] that there was a risk of losing market share if they didn't act swiftly.

REPORTING QUESTIONS

1 Reporting *yes/no* questions

We use *if* or *whether* and make any necessary tense changes:

'**Will** you be going to the reception?'	She asked me **if** / **whether** I **would** be going to the reception.
'**Did** you have a chance to speak to him?'	He wondered **if** / **whether** I **had had** a chance to speak to him.

2 Reporting open questions

When questions begin with *which, what, where, why, when, how*, etc., we report them using a different word order:

'Which airline are you using?'	She asked me which airline I was using.
'How much did you spend?'	He wanted to know how much we (had) spent.
'Who told you?'	They wanted to know who (had) told me.

The auxiliaries *do*, *does* and *did* are not used in the reported question:

'What time do you start?'	He asked me what time I started. (NOT *He asked me what time do I start.)
'How much did it cost?'	He wanted to know how much it cost. (NOT *He wanted to know how much did it cost.)
'Where is the station?'	She wanted to know where the station was. (NOT *She wanted to know where was the station.)
'When will you be leaving?'	He wondered when she would be leaving. (NOT *He wondered when would she be leaving.)

Note that there is no question mark in the reported question.

We use a reported question after a phrase like *Do you know* or *Could you tell me* to request information. In these cases a question mark is necessary:

Do you know how many people will attend?

Could you tell me if there is a phone box near here?

Have you any idea how much it costs? (NOT *Have you any idea how much does it cost?)

PRACTICE

A Sentence transformation

Report these *yes/no* questions using the words in brackets, as in the example:

1 'Do you want to call Derek?' (asked)

He asked me if I wanted to call Derek.

2 'Have you seen Bernard yet?' (asked)

....

3 'Are you open on a Saturday?' (could)

....

4 'Did you get my message?' (wondered)

....

5 'How much time is there left?' (idea)

....

6 'Will you be taking your husband with you?' (wanted to know)

....

B Enquiries

Maria works at an information desk in an airport. These are the answers she gave. Write what people asked her.

1 'The restaurant is upstairs.'

Someone asked her where the restaurant was.

2 'You can get a shuttle outside the building.'

....

3 'At the foreign exchange counter.'

....

4 'The duty free is on the first floor.'

....

5 'Yes, you can leave your suitcases in the left-luggage lockers over there.'

....

6 'I'm sorry, I really don't know why the Lufthansa flight has been delayed.'

....

REQUESTING AND OFFERING

1 Making a request

Here are some ways of making requests, according to the degree of politeness:

impolite

Get me another glass. I want another glass. Another glass, OK?

neutral

Can I have another glass, please? I'd like another glass, please.

Is it all right if I have another glass?

slightly more polite

Could I have another glass, please? May I have another glass, please?

very polite

I was wondering if I could have another glass. Could you possibly give me another glass, please?

Do you mind if I have another glass? Would you mind my having another glass?

2 Accepting a request

Yes, sure. Fine. No problem. Go ahead. Certainly.

3 Refusing a request

I'm sorry, I can't. / That's not possible. Well, I'm afraid ... (+ reason)

Note: If someone makes a request with *would you mind* and *do you mind if* and we want to say *yes,* we can say *Of course not*:

'Would you mind lending me your pen for a minute?' 'No, of course not.'

If we want to refuse, we can say *Well, (actually) I'd rather not* (+ reason):

'Could you help me move this desk?' 'Sorry, I'd rather not. I've got a bad back.'

4 Offering

Would you like to ...? Would you like me to ...? Shall I ...?

We can make a spontaneous offer using *I'll*:

'The last train has gone.' 'Don't worry. I'll give you a lift if you like.'

Accepting offers	*Declining offers*
Thank you very much.	No, that's all right, thank you.
That's very kind of you.	No, don't bother. / I can manage.

PRACTICE

A Polite requests

The following short dialogues are not very polite. Rewrite them to make them sound more acceptable.

EXAMPLES: ~~I want to~~ speak to Mrs Gosso.

Could I speak to Mrs Gosso, please?

~~She isn't here. What do you want to speak to her for?~~

I'm afraid she isn't here. Would you like to leave a message?

1 **A** I want to leave early.
B No way.

2 **A** Want a lift?
B Yes.

3 **A** Give me $50 until tomorrow.
B I haven't got any money.

4 **A** Want a glass of sherry?
B No.

5 **A** Bring me the bill.
B OK.

6 **A** Tell me the way to the station.
B No idea where it is.

B Doing someone a favour

The sentences in this dialogue between two colleagues are in the wrong order. Complete them with these expressions and number them in the correct order.

could you possibly	I was wondering if	I'm afraid	go ahead	I'll	Shall I

B Well, ... [1] I can't tomorrow. I'm not coming in to the office. ....

A .... [2] write it down for you? ....

B Yeah, ... [3]. ....

A .... [4] you could phone these people in Spain for me. My Spanish is atrocious. ....

B Sure. .... [5] do it first thing. ....

B Yes. Otherwise I'll forget! When do you want me to phone them? ....

A Well, ... [6] do it the day after tomorrow? ....

A Could I ask you a favour? ......*1*......

B No problem. Just tell me what you want me to say. ....

A Tomorrow. ....

SUGGESTING

1 *should* or *ought to*

We can use *should* or *ought to* to suggest what we think the right course of action is:

I think you **should** try a new strategy if the old one isn't working.

You **shouldn't** launch a new product without doing a market study first.

Shouldn't we ask him for his opinion?

They **ought to** simplify administrative procedures.

The government **ought to** reduce the rate of income tax.

Note that *oughtn't to* is possible but not very frequent.

2 *could*

If we think it is possible to improve a situation and want to recommend a course of action, we can use *could*:

We **could** reduce energy consumption by switching off PCs when they're not in use.

We **could** try to motivate staff by introducing a profit-sharing scheme.

3 *shall we, let's, why don't we, how about, what about*

In the same way as *had better*, the forms *shall we, let's* and *why don't we* are not followed by *to*. *How about* is followed by a verb + *-ing*:

Shall we offer them an increased discount?

Let's try to finish the meeting before 10 o'clock.

Why don't we lease equipment rather than buy it?

How about / What about leasing equipment rather than buying it?

4 The verb *suggest*

Remember that the verb *suggest* is never followed by the infinitive. These are the correct structures (the words in brackets are optional):

I **suggest** that we (should) **get** some financial advice.

I **suggest** (our) **getting** some financial advice. (NOT *I suggest to get ...)

5 *could always*

We say *could always* to suggest something that may solve a problem:

You **could always** review your reward system if you think people are losing motivation.

PRACTICE

A Making suggestions

Match the problems 1–5 with the proposed solutions a–e. Complete the solutions with these expressions.

How about ...	Shall we ...	We could ...	Well, I suggest ...

1 We need to do something about our corporate image.
2 Her salary hasn't kept pace with the cost of living.
3 How are we going to get to the meeting at head office on time if there's a transport strike?
4 Where are we going to entertain the visitors while they're here?
5 Do you have any ideas on how to improve motivation?

a) .... stay in a nearby hotel overnight?
b) .... hiring a new public relations manager?
c) .... taking them to a night club.
d) .... give people more responsibility for decision-making.
e) .... offering her some kind of promotion to a more highly-paid position?

B Problem-solving

Below are a number of problems. Make suggestions using language from page 140.

1 We don't seem to be able to keep our skilled staff. They leave after two or three years and sell their services elsewhere.
2 Some of our customers are late in making payments and we have to send them a number of reminders before we get our money.
3 We'd like to get shelf space in the major supermarket chains but we haven't been able to do so.
4 Our firm seems to have a large number of old-fashioned computers and incompatible software. We don't know what to do with it all.
5 My boss gives me far too much work and doesn't seem to understand that I also have a family life.

UNDERSTANDING SIGNS AND NOTICES

1 Giving information

OUT OF ORDER: a machine is not working

TO THE PLATFORMS: directing passengers in a train station

SOLD OUT: there are no goods left for sale

FOREIGN EXCHANGE COUNTER: in a bank; you can change currency here

2 Asking people to do things

PLEASE HAND IN YOUR KEY AT THE DESK: in a hotel lobby

EXACT FARE PLEASE: NO CHANGE GIVEN: on a bus

PLEASE PAY AT THE CHECKOUT: in a supermarket

PLEASE LEAVE YOUR TRAYS HERE: in a self-service restaurant

3 Asking people not to do things

KEEP OUT: Do not enter this property.

UNAUTHORISED VEHICLES STRICTLY FORBIDDEN: Do not park here.

DO NOT LEAVE BAGS UNATTENDED: Keep your bags with you.

4 Warning

MIND YOUR HEAD: The ceiling is low.

BEWARE OF PICKPOCKETS: Professional thieves may be around.

CROSS ONLY WHEN LIGHTS SHOW: or you may get run over.

WORKS ENTRANCE: The entrance to the factory is here.

TOLL AHEAD: You will have to pay to use this road / bridge / tunnel.

HEAVY PLANT CROSSING: Lorries, etc. come out of this entrance.

PRACTICE

A Signs and notices

Where would you see these signs and notices? Match the signs 1–13 with the places a–i.

a) in a supermarket
b) on a motorway
c) on a box of laboratory equipment
d) in a car park
e) in an airport
f) in a bank
g) in a hotel
h) in a filling station
i) in a self-service restaurant

1 FRAGILE

2 PLEASE PAY AT THE CHECKOUT

3 SERVICES 15 MILES

4 ↑ THIS SIDE UP ↑

5 SELF-SERVICE PLEASE TAKE A TRAY

6 PAY AND DISPLAY

7 PLEASE HAVE YOUR BOARDING PASS READY

8 – POSITION CLOSED –

9 CHECK YOUR TYRE PRESSURE HERE

10 PLEASE VACATE YOUR ROOM BY NOON

11 *THE MANAGEMENT CANNOT ACCEPT LIABILITY FOR GUESTS' BELONGINGS LEFT ON THE PREMISES*

12 DIVERSION AHEAD

13 EXPRESS TILL: TEN ITEMS OR FEWER

UNIT **15**

Focusing on information

ADDING AND COMBINING INFORMATION

1 Adding information

One simple way of adding extra information in writing is to separate it by dashes (–) or commas (,):

One of the dreams of laser technology – a stable blue laser operating at room temperature – is now available for scientific, commercial and personal use. Nichia Chemical Industries, a small Japanese company, demonstrated a blue laser as early as 1993.

2 Identifying people and things with relative pronouns

We use *who* or *that* to refer to people. We use *which* or *that* to refer to things:

The man **who** / **that** gave me my first job was a genius.

A modem is a device **that** / **which** sends information down the telephone lines.

To refer to places and time we use *where.* To refer to a time *we use when*:

Opposite is the National Gallery, **where** you can see many famous British paintings.

A bank holiday is a day **when** most shops and offices close.

The clauses introduced by the relative pronouns identify and define the previous nouns. The pronouns are the *subject* of the relative clause and cannot be left out.

3 Indicating possession

If a person's credit card is stolen, he / she should report it immediately.

Anyone **whose** credit card is stolen should report it immediately.

4 Combining information

Note how these two statements can be joined together into one sentence:

The group had a record turnover last year. The group is looking to continue its expansion.

The group, **which** had a record turnover last year, is looking to continue its expansion.

Which introduces extra, non-essential information and is said to be **non-defining.** We do not use *that* in non-defining clauses.

(NOT *The group, ~~that~~ had a record turnover last year, is looking to continue its expansion.)

Whose can also be used to add further information:

Vendome's sales of prestige goods depend heavily on Japanese and east-Asian consumers. Vendome has been hit by the turmoil in the region's economies.

Vendome, **whose** sales of prestige goods depend heavily on Japanese and east-Asian consumers, has been hit by the turmoil in the region's economies.

PRACTICE

A Definitions: a financial quiz

Match the words with their definitions. Complete the definitions with a relative pronoun (*that*, *which*, *where*, *who* or *whose*).

1 The over-the-counter market
2 Options
3 Floating exchange rates
4 Bears
5 A preference share
6 Names
7 A stock exchange

a) is a market .... shares and government bonds are bought and sold.
b) are investors .... believe share prices are likely to fall.
c) are wealthy individuals .... provide funds to back Lloyd's insurance policies.
d) are financial instruments .... give the right but not the obligation to buy or sell a commodity at a certain price.
e) is the market .... securities are traded outside a regular exchange.
f) are the values of currencies .... fluctuations against each other are set by market forces.
g) is a share .... guarantees holders a prior claim on dividends.

B *whose, who, which, that*

Complete the sentences with an appropriate relative pronoun.

1 Citigroup , ... bid for Wachovia failed last week, fell another 5.1 percent to $17.41.
2 Philip Coggan, ... wrote *The Money Machine*: *How the City Works*, is a journalist with the *Financial Times*.
3 The BBC World Service, ... is financed by the Foreign Office, said it intended to invest £14m ($21m) in improving its internet services.
4 The product has been produced by a well-known company .... perfumes have always been sold in the higher price ranges.
5 Ice cubes .... crackle louder according to the strength of your drink have been developed in Japan.
6 We have developed a new computerised stock control system .... will allow us to compete with our much larger rivals.

EMPHASISING

1 Using *so* and *such*

We can use certain words like *so*, *such*, *really* and *just* to provide emphasis:

'It is **so** much easier for men. They don't have to paint their nails for a meeting.' (Eve Pollard, British journalist)

My boss is **such** a boring person. (NOT *a so boring person)

Our holiday was **really** / **just** fantastic.

2 Using adjectives to provide emphasis

We can stress our feelings about something by putting one of the following adjectives in front of a noun:

absolute complete entire outright perfect positive
pure real total true utter whole

FOR EXAMPLE:

The meeting was an **utter** waste of time. The chairperson spent a **whole** hour talking **absolute** nonsense and any attempt to intervene was bound to be a **complete** failure.

3 Using adverbs to provide emphasis

We can transform the above adjectives into adverbs by adding *-ly* (with the exception of *outright*, which stays the same):

I was **absolutely** horrified.

I agree with you **entirely**.

The party was **truly** amazing.

He seems **perfectly** satisfied.

4 Emphasising a statement

We can use the following words if we want to emphasise the truth of an entire statement or stress its serious nature:

above all actually believe me indeed to put it mildly to say the least

It was an unnecessary remark, **to say the least**.

5 Emphasising a negative statement

We can use *whatsoever* or *at all* after *none* or *no* + noun to focus on a negative statement:

There's **no** need **whatsoever** / **at all** to worry.

'Do you think he stands a chance of getting the job?' **'None whatsoever** / **at all**.'

PRACTICE

A Ajaz Ahmed

Complete the text using these words.

whatsoever	to say the least	indeed	so	total	truly	whole	such

Ajaz Ahmed is a .... [1] remarkable man. He was once voted the person who had made the biggest contribution to the development of e-business in Britain. This was, ... [2], a tremendous achievement.

He left school at 16 and went to work at Dixons, the British electronic goods retail chain. At the age of 36, after being a store manager for much of his career, it became clear to him that Dixons should offer internet access. It took him a .... [3] three years to convince the board that the company should launch Freeserve, which, unlike other providers, offers access with no subscription cost .... [4].

Freeserve was a .... [5] success and was bought by the France Telecom–owned company Wanadoo for £1.65bn and rebranded as Orange. It took Stanley Kalms, the founder of Dixons, 40 years to achieve as much. .... [6], no one in Britain has ever before created .... [7] much wealth in .... [8] a short period of time.

EXPRESSING A REACTION

1 Indicating your opinion

We can use a number of adverbial expressions to indicate a point of view. They usually come at the beginning of the sentence and comment on the whole of it:

In my opinion, we should never have accepted the work in the first place.

Surprisingly, she accepted a decrease in salary without protesting.

I was once kidnapped in Afghanistan. **Luckily**, I was released the same day.

Ironically, his cold got better on the last day of his holiday.

They can, however, come after the verb *to be* like other adverbs:

Predictably, the Greens were opposed to the construction of a new power station.

The Greens were **predictably** opposed to the construction of a new power station.

We use the following adverbs to indicate attitude in this way:

absurdly admittedly coincidentally conveniently curiously fortunately incredibly
interestingly mysteriously naturally oddly paradoxically sadly significantly
typically unbelievably understandably unexpectedly unfortunately unhappily

2 Indicating your attitude

We can use the following to make our attitude clear:

in all + abstract noun	e.g. **in all** sincerity / fairness
to be perfectly + adjective	e.g. **to be** (**perfectly**) honest / fair / frank
to put it + adverb	e.g. **to put it** mildly / crudely

3 Exclamations

We use *What* + noun and *How* + adjective to make exclamations:

What a mess!	**What** a surprise!	**What** terrible weather!
How awful!	**How** amazing!	**How** nice of her!

We can also express reactions such as surprise, approval or disgust, using exclamations or short phrases. These are some of the most common:

approval:	Great! Superb! Mmm.
disapproval:	Rubbish! Nonsense! What are you talking about?
irritation:	Damn! (not polite) Oh no! Hell! (not polite)
surprise:	Wow! Gosh! You're joking!
disgust:	Ugh! Yuk! That's ghastly!

PRACTICE

A Indicating attitude

Complete the sentences using these words.

conveniently	mysteriously	typically	understandably	paradoxically

1 Decision-making .... takes longer in cultures which are community-oriented and where there are sustained efforts to achieve a consensus. In individualistic cultures it is more acceptable to vote down those who disagree.

2 ...., some businesses, for example low-priced brands, may slip from boom into bust because broad economic conditions are improving.

3 Mock job interviews are conducted at the beginning and end of each workshop. At the start, participants are .... monosyllabic, hesitant, sometimes sullen. They mumble inaudibly when asked why they should be hired, often citing as justification the fact that they 'need a job'.

4 Strange things are happening in Westminster. Some clocks have started to go backwards and Big Ben has .... stopped.

5 General Electric consists of four different divisions .... grouped under one banner but managed separately.

B Exclamations

1 **Complete the exclamations with *What*, *What a* or *How*.**

1 .... extravagant!
2 .... mess!
3 .... rubbish!
4 .... awful!
5 .... fantastic idea!
6 .... disgusting!
7 .... lucky!

2 **React to these statements with an appropriate exclamation.**

1 There are files all over the floor and piles of newspapers everywhere.
2 He spent half his monthly salary on clothes in just one day.
3 They eat the intestines of a sheep fried in fat and milk, with a chocolate sauce.
4 She won $1 million after buying her first lottery ticket ever.
5 Men and women can't possibly do the same kind of work.
6 He was going to be a pilot and then lost an eye in a road accident.
7 In polluted cities we could sell people fresh air in cans and make a fortune.

GENERALISING / INDICATING RELEVANCE

1 Generalising

If we want to say that something is true, but maybe not 100% true, we can use a general introductory word or phrase:

All in all it has been a good year despite some uncertainties.

Basically the two machines are the same but with a different exterior.

By and large we treat our employees fairly.

On the whole we work together well even if we don't always agree.

Overall, sales have been good, but not fantastic.

Other words used in this way include:

all things considered   as a rule   broadly speaking   for the most part
in general   on average   on balance   roughly speaking

2 Indicating relevance

If we want to state our field of reference, we can use certain adverbs before an adjective or at the beginning or end of a clause:

Technically, glass-making is a relatively simple process.

It's not **politically** correct to say *fireman*; you should say *firefighter*.

Aesthetically, our head office is a very fine building.

We can also use *from a / an* (adjective) *point of view*:

From a financial point of view, the idea doesn't make sense.

From an ethical point of view, hiring children would be wrong.

Some of these adverbs occur with *speaking*:

Technically speaking, England only refers to one country, not the whole of the British Isles.

Scientifically speaking, matter is just packets of quanta.

PRACTICE

A General statements

Make general statements from these prompts.

1 Charities, by ...., are exempt from income tax.
2 All ...., it's been a pretty good year for our firm.
3 On ...., life was much less stressful in the past.
4 As ...., I try not to show favouritism to any of my staff.
5 In ...., about 10% of the candidates are offered positions.

B ... *speaking*

Complete the sentences with one of these adverbs and *speaking*.

broadly	relatively	technically	aesthetically

1 ...., the building is extremely ugly, even if it is functional.
2 ...., bank managers belong to the middle class of society.
3 ...., English is an SVO (subject, verb, object) language with a relatively fixed word order.
4 Humankind is, ..., a newcomer on Earth.

C Points of view

Match the sentence halves.

1 From a military point of view,
2 From an ethical point of view,
3 From an environmental point of view,
4 From a scientific point of view,
5 From a financial point of view,

a) it is wrong to do to other people what you would not want done to you.
b) Jupiter is an extremely interesting planet.
c) it doesn't make sense to buy stocks when they've reached their peak.
d) it is better to use aircraft to bomb strategic targets before using ground troops.
e) it is better to build on 'brownfield' rather than 'greenfield' sites.

HIGHLIGHTING INFORMATION

1 Selecting

Some adverbs select a particular group of things or people from a larger group:

There is a substantial demand for employees in manufacturing, **notably** in electronics and telecommunications.

The group has £250m to spend on acquisitions and is looking **particularly** at Germany and the US.

Other adverbs used in this way include:

chiefly especially mainly mostly
predominantly primarily principally specifically

Some focusing adverbs point to one particular thing exclusively:

This offer is available **exclusively** / **solely** to our established clients.

Price **alone** is not a reliable indicator of quality.

We use *only* to refer to a person or thing to the exclusion of all others:

Only the CEO is able to make such decisions.

The car park is for authorised personnel **only**.

We use **only** the best quality ingredients.

2 Focusing on the topic

Clauses with *what* as their subject focus on the thing we are talking about.

Compare:

A You're asking for a bigger salary. B That's right.

A What you want is a bigger salary. B That's right.

In the second exchange the information introduced by *what* is old or given in the context. The bigger salary is the new or important information to focus on.

	Focus of the sentence
What we need	is a bigger budget.
What impressed me most	was his professionalism.
What you have to do	is choose the right foreign partner.
What I would like	is a long holiday.
What I will do first	is give you a brief history of the project.

3 Putting negative ideas first

When negative expressions begin a sentence, the normal order of subject and the auxiliary is reversed in order to emphasise the negative aspect:

Never before have we commissioned such an extensive survey.

Under no circumstances can we allow unauthorised visitors to enter the factory.

On no account should confidential information be shown to the press.

PRACTICE

A Highlighting information

Match the sentence halves.

1 The population of Dublin is predominantly Irish,
2 Her work as a pollster consists chiefly
3 Violent crime is growing at a rapid rate,
4 Boredom was mainly
5 Some early doctors, notably Hippocrates,
6 Linda is hoping to move to Spain,

a) especially in urban areas.
b) in interviewing members of the public.
c) or, more specifically, Toledo.
d) thought that diet and hygiene were important.
e) why I decided to quit.
f) but there are many other nationalities living there as well.

B Focusing on the topic

1 **Change the focus of the topic in these sentences, as in the example.**

EXAMPLE: I'm talking about a radical change in policy.
What I'm talking about is a radical change in policy.

a) We need a good overseas partner.

....

b) You have to have the right distribution network.

....

c) You must make sure your products are suited to the local market.

....

2 **Francis Knight is giving a presentation. Here are three things he could say during his speech in order to focus on his intentions. Rewrite them with *what*.**

EXAMPLE: I will first give you an idea of how the project started.
What I will do first is give you an idea of how the project started.

a) I will then describe the project in more detail.

....

b) I will next tell you how we defined the potential market.

....

c) I want to convince you that this project is worth investing in.

....

C Negative ideas

Rewrite these sentences to emphasise the negative aspect.

1 We have never faced such a difficult challenge.
2 You should under no circumstances handle dangerous products without protective clothing.
3 You must on no account tell him about our plans.

LINKING (1)

We use link words, especially in formal writing, to signal the kind of connection there is between one statement and another.

These extracts show how some of the major link words are used to connect ideas which are contained in different sentences.

1 Contrast

Large-scale information technology projects are notoriously difficult to control. **However**, in the case of the massive euro conversion in 1999, everything went according to plan.

When a personal computer for home use is marketed strongly on the back of powerful visual images, the prospect of playing computer games becomes an important factor for many potential buyers. **Nevertheless**, it is difficult for manufacturers to establish just how far hardware sales are driven by game-playing.

There have been many international conferences which have discussed the issue of Third World debt. **Yet** very little seems to have been achieved so far to write off loans and increase development aid.

When we want to express a clear contrast between two subjects in the same sentence we can use *whereas*:

Whereas the traditional home PC used to be a stand-alone device, today's high-powered machines are designed to be multifunctional entertainment and communication devices equally capable of running the latest 3D adventure game, surfing the worldwide web for homework or creating your own weblog.

We use *although*, *in spite of* or *despite* before a statement that makes the main statement seem surprising or unlikely:

The results, **although** modest, were better than expected.

Although the currency crisis has hit local demand, the lower value of the baht has increased the competitiveness of exports.

Despite / **In spite of** advances in automated call technology, most people want to talk to a real person, not just a disembodied voice.

Despite being so unpopular, the present administration has successfully carried out a number of reforms.

PRACTICE

A Contrasting

Underline the correct linking word in each of these paragraphs.

1 *Whereas / Although / Despite* having to wait four to five years before it is delivered to you, demand for a Stirling car is strong.

2 *Although / Despite / Nevertheless* American software firms are still well ahead of their European and Asian counterparts, the latter are catching up fast.

3 Demand and price go up and down, interest rates fluctuate, rival firms disrupt even the most carefully-laid plans, employees make mistakes. The list of potential disasters is long, that of opportunities much shorter. *In spite of / Yet / Despite* for most businesses, the rules of the game and the types of disasters or opportunities stay much the same for years, or even decades, at a time.

4 *However / Although / Nevertheless* the types of jobs for which intercultural training is considered essential – namely expatriate positions – are on the decline, the globalisation of firms has increased the need for cultural sensitivity training.

5 Many women feel that full equality in the workplace has not been achieved. *Nevertheless / Although / Whereas* most will admit that there has been progress over the last thirty years.

6 *Whereas / Nevertheless / Despite* American companies are allowed to own 49% of a European airline, European groups are limited to 25% of US carriers.

B Link words

Complete these sentences with an appropriate linking word.

1 .... the issues were important, not many people bothered to vote.

2 There is no doubt that lowering interest rates early prevents recession. ...., lowering them to cure a recession that already exists doesn't work.

3 .... making a record profit last year, the firm has decided to make 500 employees redundant.

4 Some cultures prefer meetings to start on time .... others are not bothered about punctuality.

LINKING (2)

2 Result

If PC sales – and, **therefore**, sales of the Intel microprocessors which power most of them – are to continue to grow, the PC will need to 'win the battle for the consumer's eyeballs'.

There have been rumours of a take-over bid. **As a result**, the share price has soared.

The baggage-handling equipment often doesn't work properly. **Consequently**, baggage gets stuck on the conveyor system and the system breaks down.

3 Extra information

It's fast, comfortable and safe. It's very economical, **too**.

Our firm has been investing heavily in getting more customers online. We've consulted clients widely on the design of our web pages and they have been improved over the past year. **In addition**, we have been running seminars to show our customers our services and how to make the most of them.

Advances in IT and in the globalisation of business have fostered the growth of knowledge-based companies and global brands. **Furthermore**, in many mega-mergers now, the main assets involved are often intangibles together with the resultant goodwill which often has a value of many billions of pounds.

4 Sequencing in time

Zimbabwe was **formerly** known as Rhodesia.

I'm really glad Barbara has found a job **at last**. She's been out of work for ages.

The plane **eventually** landed at 16.30, over four hours late.

The plane will be ready for take-off shortly. **Meanwhile**, please wait in the departure lounge.

Many scientific theories were **subsequently** disproved by experimental evidence.

5 Ordering points

Sixty per cent of all business plans are rejected so it's important to bear in mind a few essential points if you're thinking of submitting a proposal to investors.

First of all, your plan must be factual yet attractive. **Second**, it must not be too long and it should not be repetitive. **Third**, it should describe you, your business idea, what you need in the way of investment and what profit an investor may expect. **Next**, you should describe the product or service. Explain the advantages. Is it cheaper? Is it better quality? What is its unique feature? **Then** you should describe your market and its future prospects and define your particular niche. **Last but not least**, you will need to provide financial forecasts for the next three years, including profit and loss accounts, cash flow statements and a specimen balance sheet.

PRACTICE

A Categories of link words

Organise these words under the headings.

consequently moreover so also formerly meanwhile too subsequently on the other hand alternatively eventually thus therefore furthermore even so nevertheless

Contrast	*Result*	*Extra information*	*Sequencing in time*
....	....	....	....
....	....	....	....
....	....	....	....
....	....	....	....

B Link the statements

Link the statements in column A with those in column B.

A

1 Heathrow is one of Europe's most modern airports.

2 I would like to spend more time with my family.

3 The drug has powerful side effects.

4 The weak demand for our products in the domestic market and in Asia hit us harder than we expected.

5 She's been under a lot of pressure recently.

6 I didn't enjoy the time I spent on the production line.

B

a) **Furthermore**, it may be addictive.

b) **However**, it is severely congested.

c) **Moreover**, competition in the US and Europe is increasing.

d) **On the other hand**, it did give me first-hand experience of factory work.

e) I have **therefore** decided to resign as chairperson.

f) **As a result**, she's decided to take time off to relax a little.

SUBSTITUTING

1 *so*

To avoid repeating information we can use *so* and *not* after verbs such as *believe*, *hope*, *expect*, *guess*, *imagine*, *suppose* and *think*:

'Is Mr White in?' 'I think **so**.' (instead of repeating 'I think that he is in.')

'Will we lose money?' 'I hope **not**.' (instead of 'I hope that we will not lose money.')

We use *I'm afraid so* when we are sorry that the answer is *yes*:

'Will we lose money?' 'I'm afraid **so**.'

Negative sentences offer two alternative substitution structures:

'He won't change, will he?' 'No, I **don't** suppose **so**.' / 'No, I don't think **so**.'

'He won't change, will he?' 'No, I hope **not**.' / 'No, I'm afraid **not**.'

Hope and *afraid* are always used with the second structure (NOT *I don't hope so / *I'm not afraid so.).

I think **not**, *I believe* **not** and *I suppose* **not** are much more formal.

2 *such*

To refer back to a previously mentioned idea or statement we can use *such*:

The union wishes to introduce a 35-hour working week. I would oppose **such** a move.

'She wants to set up a utopian communist colony.' 'Where does she get **such** ideas?'

3 *this / that*

We can use both *this* and *that* to refer back to something previously mentioned:

The key to meeting today's challenges depends more than ever on recruiting the right people. But **this** / **that** is easier said than done.

However, only *this* can point forward to something that hasn't yet been mentioned:

Good evening. **This** is the news.

This is the third time I've had to ask you when I will see the test results.

4 *the former / the latter*

When two items are presented in a list, we can refer back to the first item using *the former* or the last-mentioned using *the latter*.

The Rolls Royce and the Ferrari are luxury cars. **The former** is British while **the latter** is Italian.

PRACTICE

A *so* and *not*

Answer these questions positively with the words in brackets.

EXAMPLE: Do you recognise this music? (think) ...Yes, I think so....

1 Will he be able to take the initiative? (expect)

2 Will many people attend? (imagine)

3 Do you think he'll be angry? (guess)

Now react negatively.

EXAMPLE: She won't want to leave late. (guess) ...No, I guess not....

4 Will we be getting a bonus? (afraid)

5 It isn't dangerous, is it? (hope)

6 We'd better not use it without asking. (suppose)

B Avoiding repetition

Rewrite these sentences in order to avoid any repetition.

1 I may be free this afternoon. If I am free this afternoon, I'll come and see you.

2 Africa has long had a bad reputation for business – companies investing there fear the unknown and often rightly fear the unknown.

3 A senior monetary official said that he regretted the decision not to join the Economic and Monetary Union in 1999 for one particular reason: the operational structure of the Bank of England would have made a perfect role model for the European Central Bank – much more a perfect role model for the ECB than the German Bundesbank.

C Referring

What do the words in bold type refer to?

Maybe it is luck. I have never spilt a cup of coffee over my laptop keyboard, trodden on it or dropped it down a flight of stairs. But I know people who have done **so**, and the results were not pretty.

Recognising **this**, some laptop makers, led by Japan's Panasonic (www.panasonic.com/business/Toughbook), have pioneered the concept of 'ruggedised' portable PCs suitable for use by anyone working in physically challenging environments.

Typically, fully ruggedised laptops are **those** that meet military specifications, including the ability to withstand a 3-foot drop, heavy rainfall and extreme hot and cold.

Most ruggedised laptops come with shock-protected hard drives, reinforced watertight and dustproof cases and rubber corner 'bumpers'; **the latter** are designed to enable the computer to survive a 3-foot drop.

Such engineering does not come cheap. Most fully ruggedised laptops cost more than $3,000. Recently, however, Panasonic and other PC makers including Hewlett-Packard, Dell and Lenovo have launched a class of semi-rugged laptops known as 'business-rugged'.

These are aimed at the growing number of people who rely on their laptops and need a machine that is both sturdy and relatively accident proof – without being ugly. **These machines** have lower price tags than their fully rugged counterparts.

FT

UNIT 16 Business communication skills

MANAGING A CONVERSATION (1)

1 Introducing a topic

We very often use questions as an invitation to someone to develop a conversation. For example:

Did anyone see the film on television last night?

Have you heard about the change in plan?

We can also make an obvious statement such as:

You'll never guess what happened to me yesterday.

2 Changing topic

If we want to change the direction of a conversation, we can say:

By the way, Jim phoned.

While I'm thinking about it, Jim phoned.

While we're on the subject of motivation, what kind of incentives do you offer?

This is on a completely different subject, but Jim phoned.

3 Attentive listening

When listening to another speaker, we usually react to what is being said by using various noises and expressions of encouragement and cooperation:

I see	Is that so?	mmm	oh dear	oh really
right	that's great	uh-huh	yeah	yes, of course

If we don't respond like this, we give the impression that we are not listening or are bored and the speaker may ask a question to check that we are following.

4 Echoing

A way of showing that we are listening is to repeat a key word or phrase from what the speaker has just said. For example:

A So, anyway, I said that I couldn't possibly accept 5%.

B **Five per cent?**

A Yeah, 5%. It's just not enough.

A ... and I was going to phone her before she got back from Japan.

B **Before she got back?**

A Yeah, because I needed a decision quickly.

PRACTICE

A Introducing a topic

Introduce a topic of conversation that will elicit these answers.

1 ....

Yeah, she told me yesterday.

2 ....

No, I didn't, but I heard that it was very good.

3 ....

No, I haven't. What's happening?

4 ....

No. What went wrong?

B Changing a topic

You are in conversation and would like to change the topic. What could you say to introduce your new topic?

What you hear	*What you think or want to say*
... and so James went back and got the stuff that he'd forgotten and everything turned out OK.	... did James arrange for overtime at the weekend?
... and I think that I'll probably have to go to China and see what's happening for myself.	... did you hear what happened in Beijing?
... and there seems to be a real change in spending patterns before the Christmas period so we'll probably need to think about that.	... Sandra wants to move into another section.

C Echoing

Unscramble these jumbled fragments of two conversations.

A And if you book before the end of the month you get a 10% reduction.

C Well, I thought there was something wrong with the system.

A Yeah, that's what it said on the leaflet.

D Something wrong?

B Before the end of the month?

C Yeah, but it was working all right in the morning.

MANAGING A CONVERSATION (2)

5 Following the conversation

If we are having difficulty understanding, it is appropriate to ask for repetition or clarification:

Sorry, I don't quite follow you.

What was that again?

What was that you said about ...?

I didn't get that bit about ...

6 Keeping going

In conversation we need time to plan what we are going to say. In order not to hesitate too much and allow other people to intervene before we want them to, we use short expressions to gain thinking time:

Well, as I was saying ... Anyway ... I mean ...

And that's not all ... So you see ... and as you probably know ...

If we cannot think of a precise word and want to avoid hesitation, we use vague, imprecise language such as:

a kind of ... a sort of ... ... or something it's a bit like a ... ... and stuff like that

If we do not want to lose a turn, we use rising intonation to signal that we have not finished.

7 Turn taking

We sense that someone is about to finish what they are saying when they use falling intonation:

... and so I think we've got to move fast or we're going to lose out to the competition.

In more formal contexts, such as a meeting, it is possible to claim a turn by saying:

Sorry to interrupt but ... If I may, I'd like to comment on that. Excuse me ...
If I can just come in here ...

8 Ending a conversation

The end of a conversation has to be 'negotiated' so that no one is left talking:

'Well, I think that's all for now. I'd better be going.'

'Right. So, I'll see you on Wednesday, then.'

'OK. Yeah, Wednesday. Well, I'll let you get back to what you were doing.'

'Right. OK. Have a good trip.'

'Thanks. Bye.'

'Bye.'

PRACTICE

A Keeping going

Complete the sentences using these words.

a bit like	anyway	or something	as I was saying

1 ... and she didn't like living there and had a kind of nervous breakdown ....

2 ... and I think you know when some people are speaking English it's .... having a hot potato in your mouth ...

3 Well, ... before he interrupted, we'll just have to tighten our belts.

4 I disagree with Management by Objectives because it's too tempting to set easy goals, and ...., it's a technique which has sort of gone out of date.

B Conversational acts

Match the words in bold with their functions a–e:

1 It's not really good enough, **is it**?

2 **Sorry to interrupt**, but don't you think that's a little unreasonable?

3 A 'Shall we meet again next Monday?'
B 'Yes.'
A '**Right**.'

4 ... and don't, **for heaven's sake**, believe everything you read in the press.

5 ... and he's got this thing about status and thinks that secretaries should be more than secretaries and **anyway** that's what he thinks. I think he sees them more as Personal Executive Assistants or something.

a) claiming a turn

b) stressing what the speaker says

c) keeping going

d) inviting feedback from the listener

e) acknowledging a response

NEGOTIATING

Negotiating

Negotiating involves a number of separate stages. Some useful language is given below for each stage.

1 Stating aims

What we need to decide is ...

We would like to reach agreement on ...

Let's establish some common ground.

Can we agree on an overall procedure?

What we hope to achieve is ...

We'd also like to discuss ....

2 Imposing conditions

We couldn't order that quantity **unless** you were prepared to ...

We can place a firm order only **on condition that** you pay within a week.

We can do business with you **provided that** you give us an open account.

→ *Conditionals* page 34

3 Focusing the discussion

The key issue here is ...

What we need to talk about now is ...

One thing I want to look at is ...

We now come to the most important phase of our discussion.

4 Rejecting suggestions

That really isn't on.

That's out of the question.

I can't go along with that.

I'm afraid that's not acceptable.

5 Bargaining

If we give you an extra discount, **will** you increase the size of the order?

If you offered an extended guarantee, we **could** see our way to reducing the price.

We might be able to make a concession **if** you **do** the same.

→ *Conditionals* page 36

6 Summarising

Have I got this right?

We've agreed to ...   As we agreed, you will take care of ...   and we will ...

If there are areas which you have not reached agreement on, you can say:

There are one or two outstanding points / issues we still need to discuss.

7 Ending the negotiation

I think we've covered everything.

We can shake on that.

OK. It's a deal.

PRACTICE

A Negotiating an agreement

The government is encouraging firms to reduce the length of the working week in order to encourage job creation. But the implementation of a shorter working week is not easy and involves some tough bargaining.

The conversation below is the beginning of a negotiation between an employer and a union representative. Complete the dialogue 1–4 with the missing extracts a–d. (The dialogue reads diagonally.)

Employer	*Union representative*
So we're here to reach agreement on the proposed changeover from 40 hours to a 35-hour working week.	
	1 ....
Yes, and we can only reach agreement if we pay for 35 hours rather than 40.	
	I'm afraid that's out of the question. My members cannot possibly accept a reduction in salary.
2	
	3 ....
I don't see that happening without considerable investment in new machinery.	
	4 ....

a) Well, we seem to be getting nowhere. Let's see if we can establish some common ground.

b) That may be the case, but the company couldn't survive if we paid people the same wages for fewer hours.

c) I'm sorry, but I disagree. We can make productivity gains. If fewer people did the same amount of work in 35 hours, there wouldn't be a problem.

d) Right, and the key issue is remuneration.

PRESENTING FIGURES

1 Whole numbers

We say three *hundred, six thousand, eight million*, etc. (There is no *s* at the end of these words.) BUT we add *-s* for approximate numbers:

hundred**s of** people   million**s of** dollars, etc.

For figures over 100, British English, unlike American English, uses *and* between the hundreds and the tens:

327 BrE: three hundred **and** twenty-seven; AmE: three hundred twenty-seven

653 BrE: six hundred **and** fifty-three; AmE: six hundred fifty-three

We say *one thousand* rather than *a thousand* before a number of hundreds. The word *thousand* is not followed by *and* unless the figure is less than 1,100, 2,100, etc.

1,348	one thousand three hundred and forty-eight. (NOT *one thousand and three hundred)
1,006	one thousand and six
6,087	six thousand and eighty-seven

2 Decimals

If we have to use a decimal, we say *point*. Each figure is said separately:

	0.35	0.5	6.75
BrE/AmE	zero point three five	zero point five	six point seven five
BrE	nought point three five	nought point five	
	oh point three five	oh point five	

3 Fractions

We express fractions using ordinal numbers:

a third   a quarter   a half   two-fifths   three-quarters, etc.

1:4 is pronounced *a ratio of one to four* or *one in four*.

4 Pronunciation

We pronounce many figures individually:

A Boeing 757 (seven five seven)   Flight BA 316 (three one six)

Your code number is 4215 (four two one five)

When speaking about money we say the currency unit after the figure if it is a whole number:

$75	seventy-five dollars
¥200,000,000	two hundred million yen
$75.50	seventy-five dollars and fifty cents (or seventy-five dollars fifty/seventy-five fifty)
€16.50	sixteen euros fifty cents

PRACTICE

A Saying figures aloud

Write these figures the way they are said.

1 0.45 ....
2 1.85 ....
3 $759 ....
4 ¥125m ....
5 $\frac{1}{3}$ ....
6 $\frac{2}{5}$ ....
7 1:3 ....
8 2001 ....
9 Your account number is 342 5461 ....
10 Your personal identification number is 3749 ....

B In your situation?

Answer these questions.

1 What proportion of your time do you spend in leisure activities?
2 On average, how many children are born to each couple in your country?
3 What is the average take-home pay in your country?
4 What is the present rate of interest on a bank savings account in your country?
5 What is the rate of inflation in your country?
6 What is the ratio of men to women in your workplace?

PRESENTING INFORMATION

The words and expressions below can be used for each of the stages involved in presenting factual or visual information. They are best learnt by heart as whole 'chunks'.

1 Introducing

The subject of my presentation is ...

I'd like to give you a brief overview of ...

What I'm going to talk about today is ...

The reason I am here today is to talk about ...

2 Structuring

I've divided my talk into (four) main sections ...

My presentation will be in (three) parts ...

first of all / first second third then after that last / finally

3 Referring to visuals in a presentation

As you can see from the table / pie chart / graph / flow chart / diagram / pictogram ...

June	*July*	*Aug*	*Sept*	*Oct*
32	35	33	36	37
41	41	42	45	46
19	18	19	20	21
16	15	16	18	16
33	34	31	41	31

table

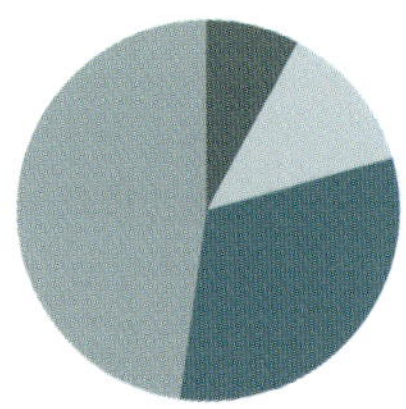

pie chart

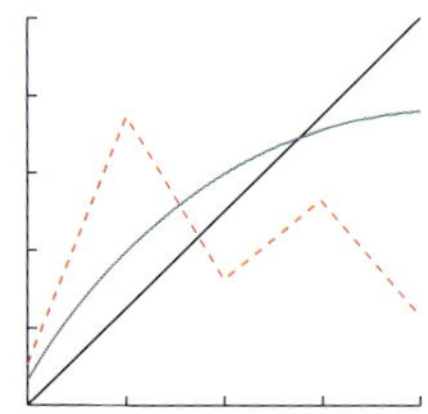

graph

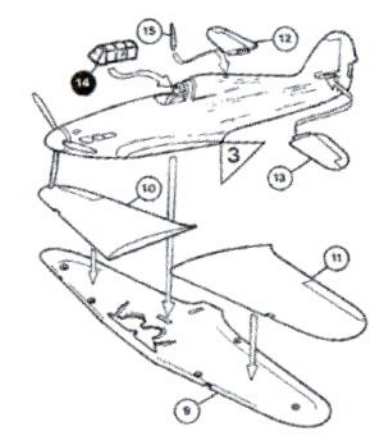

diagram

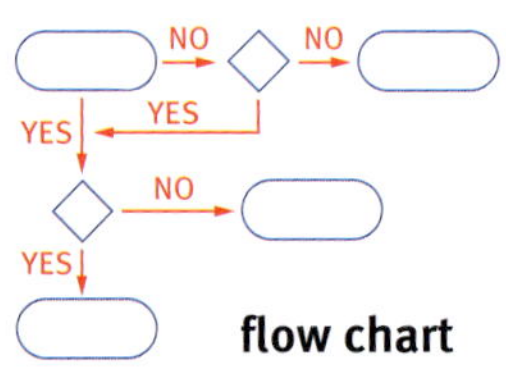

flow chart

pictogram

➡ *Presenting visual information* page 170

4 Moving on to a new point

Turning now to ...

Now I would like to describe ...

What I'd like to talk about now is ...

Now let's move on to the next point, which is ...

5 Summarising and concluding

To sum up ...

So, to go over the main points again ...

To recapitulate what I've been saying ...

I'd like to conclude by saying ...

6 Ending a presentation

Thank you for listening to me.
If there are any questions, I'll be pleased to answer them.

PRACTICE

A Presenting a company

The text below is part of a presentation of a glass-making company. Complete it with appropriate language from the box.

First	Then	third	second	If you look at	So, to recapitulate
And to complete the picture,	Now I would like to describe				
As you can see from the slide,	I'd like first of all to give you an overview				

- Good morning, ladies and gentlemen. ....[1] of our company, Pilkington Glass.
- Pilkington is organised in three worldwide business lines. ....[2], the Building products business, ...[3] the Automotive products business and ....[4] the Technical Glass products business.
- ....[5] the Building products business accounts for about half the group's sales and has manufacturing operations in 19 countries. Its largest operation is in Europe and we also have major operations in North and South America and Australasia.
- The Automotive products business represents around 45 per cent of sales. Its organisation is subdivided into two major units supplying original equipment and replacement glass. There are operations in 18 countries with a major presence in Europe and North America and important operations in South America and Australasia.
- ....[6] the Technical Glass products business accounts for the remaining sales and is centred in Germany, the United Kingdom, the United States and Italy. It manufactures glass for the electronic and optical industry, precision mirrors and solar energy panels.

  ....[7] the company's structure. ....[8] the organisation chart, the various businesses report through their management boards to the chief executive.

  ....[9], working from the corporate centre are Group functions – responsible for directing the businesses in their respective disciplines such as corporate affairs, environment and safety, finance, purchasing, legal and secretarial, human resources and internal audit. Technology is the only function that is organised centrally.
- That's all I want to say at this point on company structure. ....[10], we have three major business lines, Building products, Automotive products and Technical Glass products. And there are various Group functions that report to the chief executive through the management boards. Are there any questions at this stage?

PRESENTING VISUAL INFORMATION

1 Graphics

It is easy to produce tables, graphs, charts and diagrams to illustrate number-based information thanks to word processing software and desktop publishing packages.

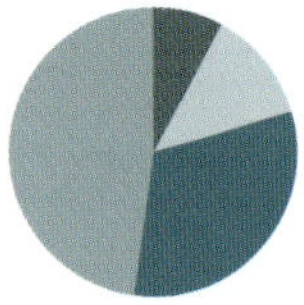

June	*July*	*Aug*	*Sept*	*Oct*
32	35	33	36	37
41	41	42	45	46
19	18	19	20	21
16	15	16	18	16
33	34	31	41	31

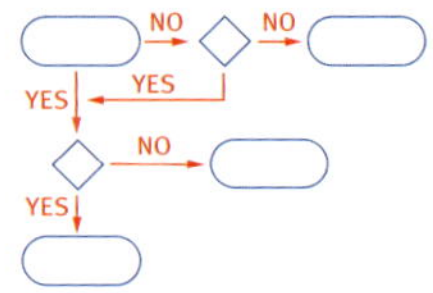

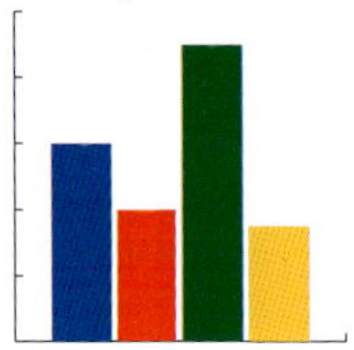

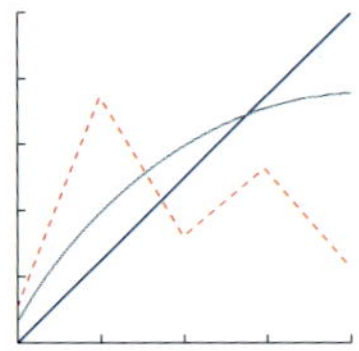

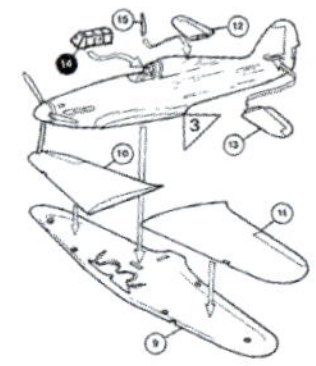

Pie charts

A pie chart has good visual impact but does not show movement.

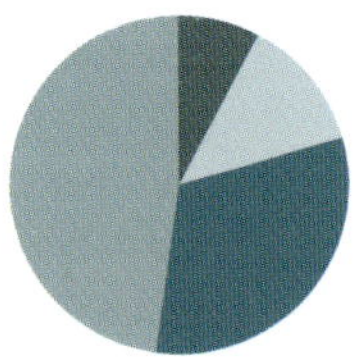

Bar charts

Bar charts can be presented vertically or horizontally. They are particularly good for making comparisons.

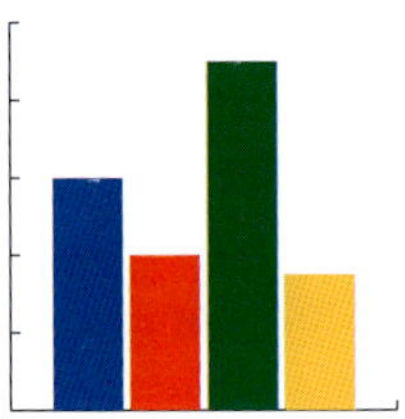

Tables

Tables give very precise information, but their visual impact is poor and they should be avoided during presentations as they may be difficult to read.

TOURIST RATES

Currency	Rate: £1 buys
Brazil (real)	2.716
China (yuan renminbi)	10.1693
Czech (koruny)	26.9516
Denmark (kroner)	8.0615
Euro	1.103
Hungary (forint)	283.679

PRESENTING VISUAL INFORMATION

Flow charts

Flow charts are used to illustrate the stages in a process. The branches show when a decision has to be made.

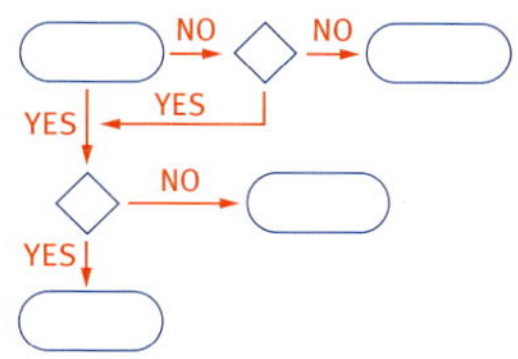

Graphs

Graphs are good for showing movements and how one thing varies against another.

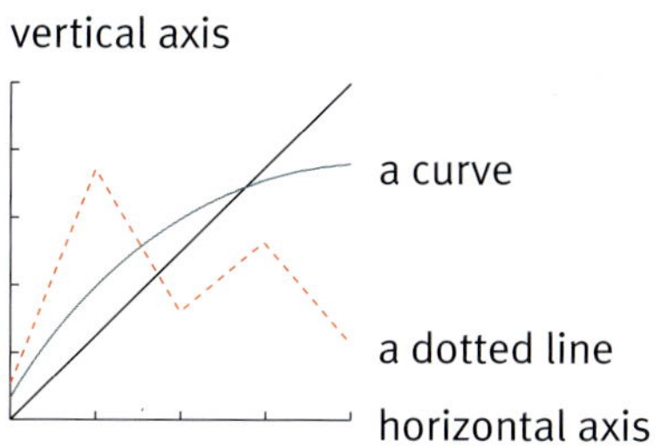

Diagrams

A diagram is an illustration designed to show how a machine or system functions.

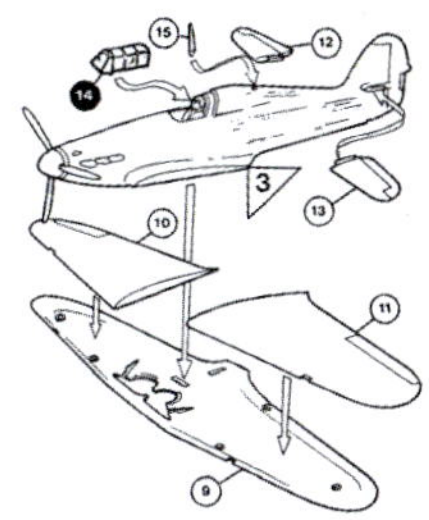

2 Describing a graph

It is not necessary to describe every single movement on a graph; an outline of the main trends is enough:

This graph shows a steady increase in the demand for oil rising steadily at the rate of 1.6% a year from 2005 to 2016. This uninterrupted growth matches the production and supply of crude oil until 2013 when it begins to fall off, reaching the same level in 2016 as that of 2006. The oil crunch begins in 2013 when demand begins to overtake supply.

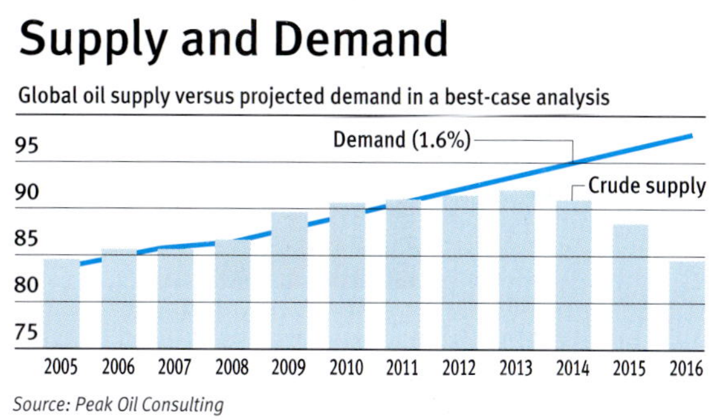

Intransitive verbs of movement:

Up	***Down***
to rise	to fall
to rocket	to plummet / to slump
to edge up	to dip
to pick up	to go down (NOT *to pick down)
to grow / recover	to decline

Note: Some verbs are transitive and need an object. For example:

to raise (prices, taxes)	to boost (the economy, sales)

PRACTICE

A

Illustrations

Label the visuals with these words.

bar chart   curve   diagram   dotted line   flow chart   graph
horizontal axis   pie chart   table   vertical axis

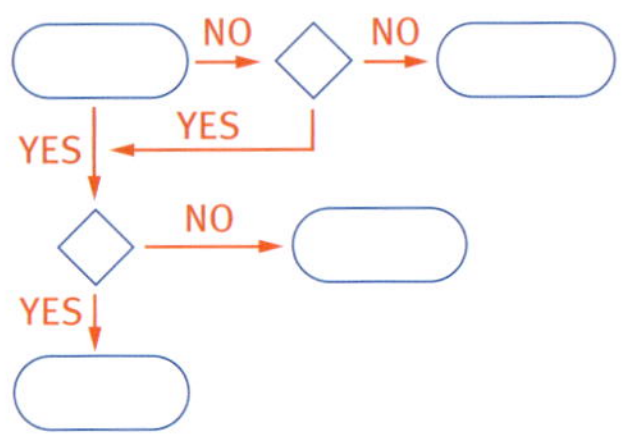

1 ....

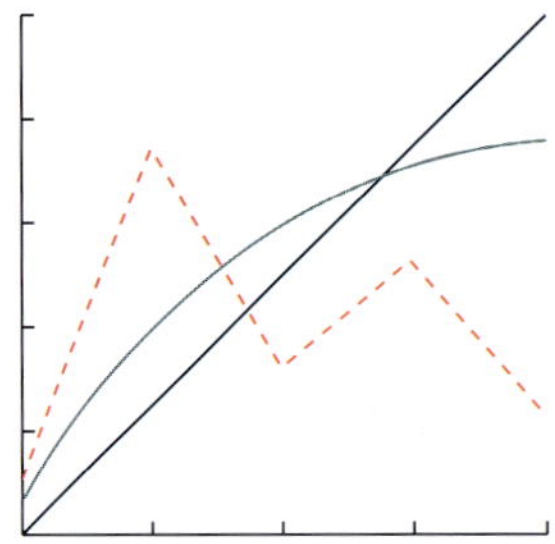

2 ....

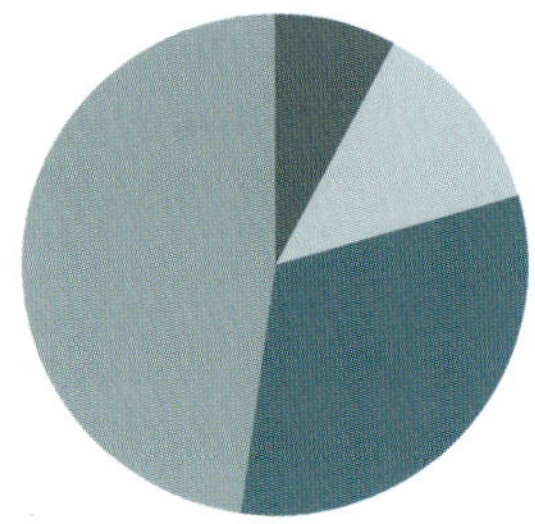

3 ....

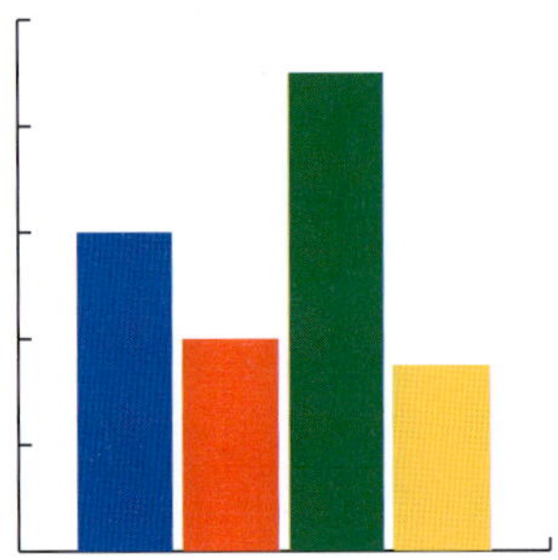

4 ....

June	July	Aug	Sept	Oct
32	35	33	36	37
41	41	42	45	46
19	18	19	20	21
16	15	16	18	16
33	34	31	41	31

5 ....

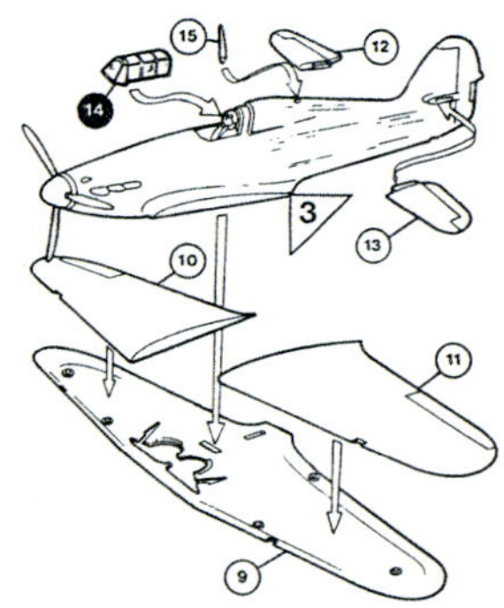

6 ....

7 ....

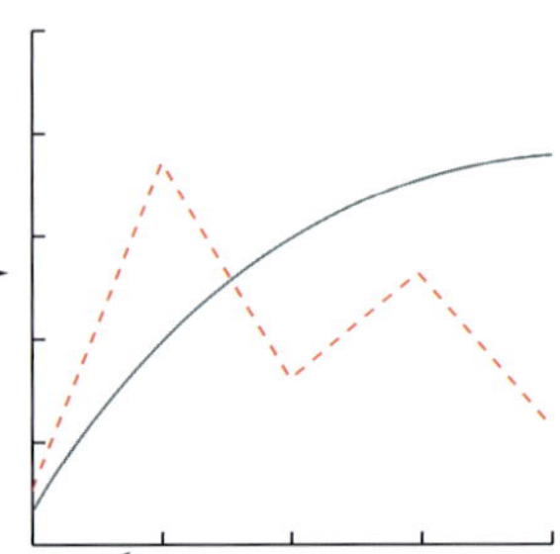

8 ....

9 ....

10 ....

PRACTICE

B

Describing graphs

1 Complete the paragraph with these prepositions.

of	to	by	at	under	from

At the end of April, sales stood ....[1] $150 million, having risen ....[2] a previous low point ....[3] just ....[4] $100 million. Over the next couple of months they rose steadily to reach a peak ....[5] $190 million. They then fell sharply ....[6] $35 million towards the end of July but crept up again in August ....[7] $160 million.

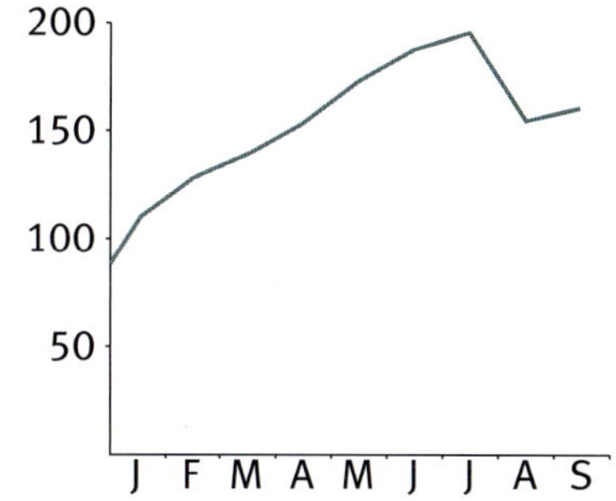

2 Write a paragraph to accompany each of the graphs below.

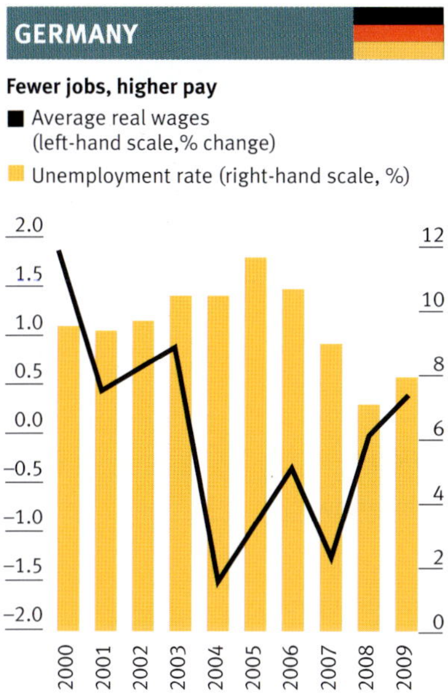

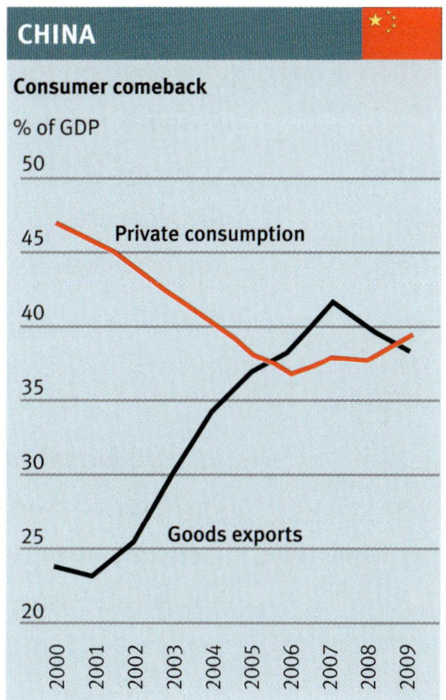

Average real wages in Germany declined ...

SOCIAL INTERACTION

1 Saying hello

To friends: Hi! Hello! Morning! How're you doing?

In more formal situations: Good morning. Good afternoon. Good evening.

Note: Only say *Good night* if you are saying goodbye in the evening.

2 Introducing yourself

My name's ... I'm ... Let me introduce myself. My name is ... (more formal)

3 Introducing others

This is ... I'd like you to meet ... Do you know ...? Have you met ...?

If you are introduced to someone for the first time who says *How do you do*? the response is *How do you do*?

4 Polite responses

Saying thank you

It is best to reply when someone thanks you for doing something or giving something.

Thanks	*Possible response*
You've been very helpful.	Don't mention it.
I appreciate your help.	My pleasure.
Thank you for your help.	You're welcome.
Thanks for the ride.	Any time.

Saying goodbye

To a friend	*In more formal situations*
I'd better be going. See you.	I'm afraid I have to leave now.
See you later / soon / some time.	I must be on my way.
Take care.	It was very pleasant meeting you.
All the best.	Enjoy the rest of your stay.
Mind how you go.	I look forward to seeing you again.

5 Reacting to what people say

We can use the following words and expressions in these situations:

When you don't hear something clearly: Sorry, I didn't catch that.

When you think something is fantastic: Wow!

If you think something doesn't matter very much: Never mind.

To ask how or why something has happened: How come?

When someone says something you find difficult to believe: You're joking!

To compliment or offer good wishes to someone: Congratulations!

PRACTICE

A Reacting to what people say

Match the expressions from the box with the thoughts behind them 1–5. Then use the expressions to complete the responses a–e.

Oh dear!	I didn't quite catch that.	Never mind.	How come?	You're joking!

1 That seems absurd.

2 I didn't understand what you just said.

3 I don't understand how this thing happened.

4 It doesn't matter; it's not terribly important.

5 I sympathise with you.

a) 'And the deal fell through even though we were 100% sure of getting the order.' '...'

b) 'I think I've erased your file.' '.............................., I've got a backup copy.'

c) 'Well, I suggest we invite the President of the United States to open the new canteen.' '.............................'

d) 'I think I've erased my file and I haven't got a backup copy.' '.............................'

e) 'cantchergettertedoitnow?' '...'

B Conversational pairs

Match the sentences 1–10 with the responses a–j.

1 I'm getting married in the spring.
2 Thanks for the ride.
3 How do you do?
4 How're you doing?
5 I'll get another round of drinks.
6 Thank you for a wonderful time.
7 Here's to a successful partnership!
8 We made over a million bucks in five days.
9 You're joking!
10 Bye then.

a) It was my pleasure.
b) Fine, thanks.
c) Wow!
d) No, it's true, I assure you.
e) Yeah, take care.
f) No, this one's on me.
g) Any time.
h) How do you do?
i) Congratulations.
j) Cheers!

TAKING PART IN MEETINGS

Some common expressions used in meetings are given below.

1 Opening a meeting

Thank you for coming.

Let's make a start, shall we?

Shall we begin?

You've all received a copy of the agenda.

The first item on the agenda is ...

James, would you like to start?

2 Stating the purpose of a meeting

The aim of this meeting is to discuss ...

What we are here to talk about is ...

We need to reach a decision on ...

3 Beginning the discussion

The first point that needs mentioning is ...

If I can just fill you in with the background to this ...

4 Calling on a speaker

Would anyone like to comment?

Paula, what do you feel?

I'd like to ask Dennis for his view.

Janet, do you have anything to add at this point?

5 Moving on to another topic

I'd like now to move on to ...

The next item on the agenda is ...

Can we go on to think about ...?

The next thing we have to discuss is ...

6 Checking everyone agrees

Do we all agree?

Is that unanimous?

Are we all happy about that?

Is that decided then?

7 Summarising decisions taken

So, what I think we've said is that ...

To recap ...

So, to sum up ...

8 Concluding the meeting

Is there any other business?

I think we've covered everything.

That's it then.

I declare the meeting closed.

That brings the meeting to a close.

Is that unanimous?

PRACTICE

A Chairing a meeting

Match the functions 1–8 with the way they can be expressed a–h.

1 opening a meeting
2 stating the purpose of a meeting
3 beginning the discussion
4 moving on to another topic
5 checking everyone agrees
6 concluding the meeting
7 summarising decisions taken
8 calling on a speaker

a) Let's move on to the next item on the agenda.
b) Perhaps Mrs Beck can tell us something about ...
c) So, what we've decided today is to ...
d) Shall we make a start?
e) Thank you for coming and for your contributions.
f) Is that to everybody's satisfaction?
g) We're here today to talk about ...
h) I'd like you in turn to give your points of view.

B Taking part in a meeting

Match the functions 1–6 with the way they can be expressed a–f.

1 interrupting someone
2 making a point strongly
3 asking for clarification
4 agreeing
5 disagreeing
6 expressing a doubt

a) Sorry, I don't quite follow you. Could you be more specific?
b) I'm not entirely sure that ...
c) That suits me fine.
d) I'm afraid I can't go along with that.
e) I do think it's important to ...
f) If I could just come in here.

TELEPHONING

1 Answering the phone

The person who answers the phone always starts the conversation.

In formal or business situations you usually give your name or the name of the company:

Hello, Mary Wells speaking.

Good morning. IKI Industries. How may I help you?

2 Stating the reason for a call

Hello. My name's ...	I'm ringing about ...
I'm ringing to ...	I'm phoning because ...

3 Leaving and taking messages

Can I leave him a message?	I'll pass that on to her.
Can I give him a message?	Could you ask her to get back to me?

4 Asking for repetition

Sorry, I didn't quite catch that. Could you repeat that, please? Could you speak up a little?

5 Taking down addresses and telephone numbers

When writing or dictating an address, you need to know how to pronounce the letters of the alphabet. The individual letters are pronounced with the same vowel sound as the words on the left.

sp**ea**k /iː/	B, C, D, E, G, P, T, V, Z (pronounced *zee* in American English)
t**e**ll /e/	F, M, N, S, X, Z (pronounced *zed* in British English)
w**ai**t /eɪ/	A, H, J, K
thr**ou**gh /uː/	U, W
ph**o**ne /əʊ/	O
l**i**ne /aɪ/	I, Y
c**a**rd /ɑː/	R

Telephone numbers are pronounced in groups. The groups usually correspond to a particular coding system (e.g. 0775 could be the area code). The digits are said separately, but in British English a repeated number can be said as *double x*. For example:

double zero	three one	seven zero three five	double four six seven eight
00	31	7035	44678
International	The Netherlands	The Hague	the number

6 Ending a call

Informal: Thanks for your call. Bye now.

Formal: Thank you for your call. / Thank you very much. Goodbye.

PRACTICE

A A phone conversation

The sentences in this conversation are in the wrong order. Number them in the correct order. The first one has been done for you.

..... I'll sign them this afternoon and send them back to you.

..... Hello. My name's Beata Szlachetka. I'd like to speak to Katie Chapman, please.

..1.. Good morning. IKI Industries. How may I help you?

..... Hold the line, please. I'll see if she's in.

..... Great. Thanks a lot.

..... (pause) Hello. Katie Chapman speaking.

..... Beata Szlachetka and I'd like to speak to Katie Chapman.

..... Hello. This is Beata.

..... Sorry, I didn't quite catch that.

..... Hi, Beata. How are you doing?

..... OK. Busy as usual.

..... Fine, thanks. And you?

..... Yeah, they came this morning but I haven't signed them yet.

..... I'm just ringing to find out if you've received the copies of the contract.

..... OK, there's no rush.

B Telephone language

Look at these expressions which are often heard or used when telephoning. Decide which are from recorded messages and mark them with X.

1 Sorry to keep you waiting.
2 Pearson Travel. Christine speaking. How may I help you?
3 I'll get him to call you back as soon as possible.
4 Hold on a moment and I'll put you through.
5 Could you put me through to the accounts department, please?
6 Could you speak up a little?
7 We are unable to take your call at the present time. Please leave your name and number after the tone.
8 This is the Australian Embassy visa information line. The consulate section is open every morning from 10 o'clock to 1 o'clock.

C Taking someone's name

Complete the sentences with the names of the people.

1 My name's ....; I'll spell that for you – gee are ay aitch ay em new word aitch you gee aitch ee es.

2 My name's ....; that's jay ay en i see ee new word why oh you en gee.

THE LANGUAGE OF CONTRACTS

Most contracts follow a pattern consisting of a number of sections and standard formulations.

DISTRIBUTORSHIP AGREEMENT, JOINT VENTURE AGREEMENT

Parties:

This distributorship agreement is made as of 25 November 2010 (the 'Effective Date') by and between O'DONNELL DISTRIBUTION, a company organised under the laws of Ireland and having its principal place of business at (address) and TOYS4U, an American Corporation, with its principal place of business at (address).

Statement of purpose:

WHEREAS O'Donnell desires to obtain sole and exclusive rights from Supplier to distribute and sell the Products (as defined herein) to Approved Customers (as defined herein) in the Territory (as defined herein), and Supplier desires to grant such rights, on the terms set forth below.

Definitions:

For the purpose of this Agreement the term "Trademarks" shall include any word, name, symbol, colour, designation or device or any combination thereof, including any trademark, trade name, brand name, logo or business symbol.

Operative provisions:

NOW, THEREFORE, in consideration of the mutual covenants and conditions herein contained, and intending to be legally bound hereby, the parties mutually agree as follows:

Termination:

This Agreement shall take effect on the Effective Date and shall expire on 31 December 2013, and the term shall automatically be extended by one (1) year unless one Party gives notice to the other Party prior to 1 July 2013 of its desire not to have this Agreement extended.

Either party may terminate forthwith by written notice if the other breaks any material term or condition and fails to remedy the breach within 30 days notice requiring the said breach to be remedied.

Applicable Law:

This Agreement shall be governed by and construed and enforced in accordance with the laws of the Republic of Ireland.

WHEREAS: Considering that.

herein: *Here* is used in legal documents to refer to the document itself and is combined with different prepositions: *herein* (in this document); *hereafter* (below); *hereby* (by this document).

sole and exclusive rights: Lawyers have to make sure that nothing is omitted in a contract. They therefore use long lists and words of similar meanings joined by *and* – terms and conditions, null and void, power and authority, goods and chattels, covenants and agrees, heirs and assigns, etc.

set forth: Written down.

shall: In legal language *shall* means 'must'.

thereof: *There* is used in legal documents to mean 'that previously mentioned thing'. Other combinations include *in respect thereof* (regarding that); and *thereto* (to that).

covenants: A covenant is an agreement to do or not to do something, e.g. a covenant not to compete.

legally bound: A contract is **binding** if it legally forces you to **comply with** (= obey) its provisions.

hereby: See *herein*.

the parties: The companies or persons signing the agreement.

expire: Come to an end. The noun is *expiry*.

the term: The duration.

prior to: Before.

forthwith: Immediately.

material term or condition: Important provision that must be performed.

breach: Failure to carry out the terms of the agreement.

said: Previously mentioned.

construed: Interpreted. The noun is *construction*.

PRACTICE

A A contract

Use the following words and expressions to complete the contract.

breach	covenant	construed	forthwith	~~herein~~	Parties
said	set forth	shall	terms	terms and conditions	WHEREAS

This ADVERTISING SALES REPRESENTATION agreement is dated as of April 3, 2011, (the "Effective Date") by and between Magpie Online Advertising Network, Inc., a California corporation (referred to ...herein... as "Magpie") and National Industrial Company, a company organized under the laws of the United Arab Emirates, referred to together as the "..................[1]".

..................[2] each Party desires to set forth in this Agreement the principal ....[3] according to which Magpie will provide certain advertising services to National Industrial Company.

1 Definitions

"Commissions" means the amount owed to Magpie in consideration for the Retail and Wholesale Services as ....[4] in Section 5.01(a) and Section 5.01(b), respectively.

"Invoice Amount" means amounts due from advertisers and sponsorship partners for services.

NOW, THEREFORE, the Parties hereby ....[5] and agree as follows:

2 Subject to the terms and conditions of this Agreement, Magpie agrees to provide or cause to be provided to National Industrial Company, and National Industrial Company agrees to purchase from Magpie, the ....[6] services until the obligation to provide the services is terminated.

3 Except as otherwise agreed in writing by the Parties, this Agreement ....[7] have an initial term from the Effective Date until April 2, 2012, and be renewed automatically thereafter for successive six-month ....[8].

Either party may terminate this Agreement ....[9] by notice in writing at any time in the event of a ....[10] by the other party for any of the reasons set out in section 10.

...

12 This Agreement shall be ....[11] in accordance with and governed by the laws of the State of California.

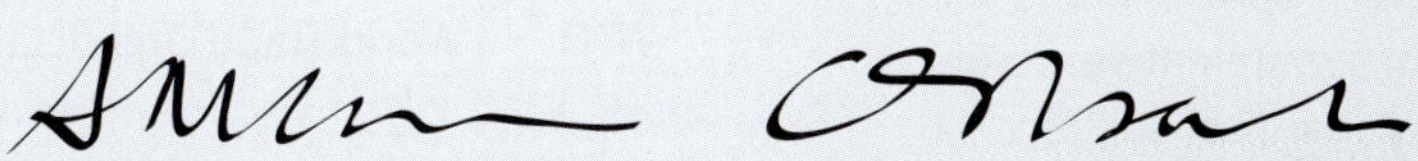

IN WITNESS WHEREOF, the Parties have caused this Agreement to be signed by their duly authorized representatives.

ABBREVIATIONS

An abbreviation is a short form of a word or expression. The letters are pronounced separately. For example, an ATM is an automated teller machine, also known as a cashpoint.

People and functions

CEO Chief Executive Officer
CFO Chief Financial Officer
CIO Chief Information Officer
COO Chief Operating Officer
HR Human Resources
MD Managing Director
PA Personal Assistant
PR Public relations
R&D Research and development
VIP Very important person
VP Vice-President

Management

AGM Annual general meeting
AOB Any other business
ASAP As soon as possible
BPR Business process re-engineering
CRM Customer relationship management / marketing
JIT Just in time
MBO Management by objectives
O&M Organisation and methods
PERT Programme / project / performance evaluation and review technique
TQM Total quality management

Manufacturing

CAD Computer-aided design
CAM Computer-aided manufacturing
SOP Standard operating procedure
The Five-Ss /faɪv esɪz/ sort, systematise, scrub, standardise, sustain

Technology

EDI Electronic data interchange
FAQ Frequently asked questions
ICT Information and communication technology
ISP Internet service provider
K One thousand (e.g. a salary of $75K = $75,000)
LCD Liquid crystal display
OHP Overhead projector
OHT Overhead projector transparency
PDA Personal digital assistant
PIN Personal identification number

Sales and marketing

B2B Business to business
B2C Business to customer
POS Point of sale
USP Unique selling proposition
The 4 Ps product, price, promotions, place

Economics and Commerce

ASEAN Association of South-East Asian Nations
EU European Union
GDP Gross domestic product
GNP Gross national product
NAFTA North American Free Trade Agreement
NGO Non-governmental organisation
NIC Newly industrialised country
OECD Organisation for Economic Co-operation and Development
UCC Uniform commercial code
WTO World Trade Organisation

Acronyms

An acronym is a word made up from the first letters of a name or phrase describing something such as an organisation. It is pronounced as a word. For example, NATO is an acronym for the North Atlantic Treaty Organization.

BENELUX	Belgium, Netherlands, Luxembourg
Bogof	Buy one get one free
EMU	European Monetary Union
GATT	General Agreement on Tariffs and Trade
ISO	International Organization For Standardization
LIBOR	London Interbank Offered Rate
NAFTA	North American Free Trade Agreement
NICs	Newly Industrializing Countries
Ninja	No income, no job, no assets
OPEC	Organization of Petroleum Exporting Countries
RoRo	Roll-on roll-off
UNCTAD	United Nations Conference on Trade and Development
Wysiwyg	(pronounced wizziwig) What you see is what you get

Miscellaneous

a/c	account
asap	as soon as possible
asst	assistant
cert	certificate
enc	enclosure
eta	estimated time of arrival
fyi	for your information
i.e.	that is to say
imo	in my opinion
jit	just in time
n/a	not applicable
NB	nota bene (note)
o/b	on or before
obo	or best offer
ono	or nearest offer
pcm	per calendar month
pls	please
pp	per pro (signed on behalf of)
PS	postscript
Sec.	secretary
thx	thanks
w/o	without
xtn	extension

Answer key

UNIT 1

Present simple (1) *page 7*

A **Mission statements**

1 welcome 2 spend 3 lead 4 come 5 means 6 depends 7 introduce 8 improve 9 work 10 stay 11 enables 12 delivers 13 strive 14 cultivates 15 endeavours 16 acknowledges 17 gives 18 fosters 19 help

B **General truths**

1 buy; put 2 talks; say 3 means 4 promise 5 tends 6 believe; believe

Present simple (2) *page 9*

A **A travel booking**

1 need 2 starts 3 Do … want 4 depends 5 does … cost 6 is 7 gets 8 takes 9 leaves 10 arrives 11 do … have to 12 do … make

B **A summary of a report**

1 focuses 2 highlights 3 provides 4 recommends 5 calls for

C **Headlines**

1 f 2 e 3 a 4 c 5 b 6 d

Present continuous (1) *page 11*

A **Events in progress**

Specimen answers

1 A man is typing on a laptop.
2 A film crew is making a documentary.
3 Some people are working in a factory.
4 A woman is welcoming a visitor.
5 A woman is making a presentation.
6 A man is buying something / paying for something with a credit card.

B **News in brief**

1 d 2 b 3 a 4 e 5 c

C Temporary situations

Specimen answers

1 ... more people are using their cars.

2 ... she's having to deal with a lot of extra work.

3 ... we're living in a bit of a mess.

4 ... I'm changing all my money into dollars.

Present continuous (2) *page 13*

A Changes

Specimen answers

1 The government is taxing companies that pollute the environment.

2 The government is putting up the rate of income tax.

3 The government is changing the law relating to working conditions.

4 The minister of transport is inaugurating a new underground line.

5 The government is closing down schools.

6 The government is building more hospitals.

B Arrangements

Specimen answers

1 'm visiting our London office.

2 'm seeing a new customer

3 'm not doing

C Present simple or present continuous?

1 PS 2 PC 3 PS 4 PS 5 PC 6 PS 7 PC 8 PS 9 PC 10 PS

a) 2 b) 3/6 c) 5 d) 7 e) 6 f) 10 g) 8 h) 4 i) 9 j) 1

UNIT 2

Past simple *page 15*

A Important firsts

2 The Wright brothers made the first flight in 1903.

3 Neil Armstrong landed on the surface of the moon in 1969.

4 Pierre and Marie Curie discovered radium in 1902.

5 Gutenberg invented the printing press in 1434.

6 Isaac Singer patented the first commercial sewing machine in 1851.

B **The Dell story**

1 began 2 introduced 3 said 4 opened 5 had 6 went 7 employed 8 totalled 9 decided 10 ran 11 launched 12 became 13 expanded 14 overtook 15 stepped down 16 stayed 17 won

C **An annual report**

1 improved 2 made 3 hindered 4 chose 5 gave

Past continuous *page 17*

A **The reasons why**

2 the fire bell was ringing.
3 their value was plummeting.
4 the president was speaking.
5 my work was suffering.
6 customers were complaining.

B **Jeff Bezos**

1 c 2 f 3 e 4 d 5 b 6 a

Past perfect simple *page 19*

A **Susan George's CV**

1 had obtained 2 had spent 3 had been 4 had developed 5 had marketed

B **Regrets**

1 had got 2 had obtained 3 had done 4 had lasted

Past perfect continuous *page 21*

A **Previous and subsequent events**

1 had been; had been waiting
2 had been working
3 had seen; had not impressed
4 had been falling
5 had been hiding
6 had been stealing
7 had been looking

B **Marcel Bich**

1 had created
2 had studied / had been studying
3 had been selling
4 had studied / had been studying
5 had been working

UNIT 3

Present perfect simple (1) *page 23*

A **India and China**

1 Have we been 2 has had 3 was 4 has India changed 5 took place 6 have had 7 has taken 8 have remained 9 previously associated 10 have been 11 has specialised 12 has always had 13 has never chosen 14 has pursued

B **Market news in brief**

1 has announced 2 have slumped 3 issued 4 has launched 5 launched

Present perfect simple (2) *page 25*

A **Previous experience**

1 Has he ever been in charge of a team?
Yes, he was in charge of a team at Steelcase Strafor.

2 Has he ever set up a business?
Yes, he set up an import company between 2005 and 2007.

3 Has he ever had direct sales experience?
No, he hasn't, but he has planned roadshows for the launch of new products.

4 Has he ever used Excel?
Probably, because he has used Microsoft Office.

5 Has he ever organised exhibitions?
No, he hasn't, but he has organised roadshows.

6 Has he ever dealt with export procedures?
Yes, he has dealt with customs clearance.

B **Time words**

Used with the present perfect	*Used with the past simple*
yet	ago
so far	yesterday
lately	at 3 o'clock
since last year	
over the last two years	
for the past three weeks	
since 2007	

1 already 2 over the past three years 3 two years ago

Present perfect continuous *page 27*

A **Recent activities**

Specimen answers

1 I've been working on a new database.

2 I've been working with a team of consultants.

3 I've been trying to find a house nearer to my place of work.

B **The effects of recent events**

Specimen answers

1

b) Some members of staff have been stealing them.

c) Someone has been leaking information to the press.

d) The chemicals plant has been discharging waste into the river.

e) She's been having Spanish lessons.

2

a) How long have you been waiting?

b) I've played tennis four times this week.

c) Look outside. It's been raining; the pavement's still wet.

d) 'You look tired.' 'I've been driving all day long.'

e) I've known John since we were at school together.

f) The government has announced a drop in unemployment.

g) I've been reading a book on negotiating skills but I don't think I'll finish it.

h) He's been working as a consultant for three different firms in the same sector of activity; I think there's a conflict of interest and he should resign.

i) He has worked as a consultant for three different firms in the same sector of activity but was fired from the first two.

j) International phone call rates have been falling for the past two years and the trend shows no sign of reversing.

UNIT 4

Future (1) *page 29*

A **Ambitions**

1 Susan is going to be a pilot.

2 Linda is going to be a racing driver.

3 Elizabeth is going to be a doctor.

4 Michael is going to be a police officer.

5 Karen is going to be an astronaut.

6 Sean is going to be a disc jockey.

B **Predictions**

1 c 2 d 3 b 4 a

Future (2) *page 31*

A **Making offers**
Specimen answers

1. I'll open a window.
2. I'll have a look at it for you.
3. I'll give you a hand.
4. I'll give you a lift.
5. I'll help you do them if you like.

B **Schedules**

1. What time does flight no. AZ 1269 arrive in Naples?
2. How long does the flight from Rome to Rimini take?
3. What time does flight no. AZ 7272 from Rome to Rimini leave?

C **Future perfect or future continuous?**

1. will have landed
2. will have disappeared
3. will be eating
4. will have become
5. will be living

Future (3) *page 33*

A **Travel arrangements**

1. 'll (will) be staying
2. 'll (will) be exploring
3. visiting
4. 'll (will) be taking
5. 'll (will) be visiting
6. 'll (will) be returning
7. (will) be transferring

B ***if*, *when*, *until*, *as soon as***

1. I'll get / I'll be getting; return
2. shut down; will lose / will be losing
3. won't start; is
4. sees / has seen
5. will go ahead / will be going ahead / is to go ahead; receives / has received

C **Announcements**
Specimen answers

1. Brussels to improve rights for consumers
2. China and EU to revive talks

UNIT 5

Conditionals (1) *page 35*

A **It's generally the case**

1 f 2 e 3 b 4 c 5 g 6 d 7 a

B **Future consequences**
Specimen answers

1 If my car is stolen, I will report it to the police.
2 If a close colleague gets married, I'll buy him/her a wedding present.
3 If I am offered a better-paid job abroad, I may accept.
4 If my firm is taken over by a competitor, I may be moved to another department.
5 If I have to give a presentation in English, I'll ask my English teacher for help.
6 If my computer is infected with a virus, I'll call an expert for assistance.

C ***if / unless***

1 If 2 unless 3 If 4 If 5 Unless 6 unless 7 if 8 If

Conditionals (2) *page 37*

A **Imagining**
Specimen answers

1 If the world was governed by a Communist superpower, people would not have the same freedom.
2 If my husband/wife was offered a good position in Iceland, I would probably refuse to go.
3 If I stood for the presidential elections, I wouldn't get through the first round.
4 If the sale of alcohol was banned in Europe, there would be fewer road accidents.
5 If I were accused of selling my country's military secrets, I would be sent to prison pending trial.

B **Bargaining**

2 give; 'll put in
3 'll take; take off
4 'll purchase; throw in
5 will you hold; order
6 pay; will you allow

C **Negotiating positions**

2 If we made a repeat order, would you agree to split the transport costs 50–50?
3 If we ensured free maintenance, would you buy a new photocopier from us?
4 If I bought the turbo-diesel model, would you install air conditioning and a GPS free of charge?

D ***provided (that), so long as, on condition (that)***
Specimen answers

1 on condition that I'm paid treble time for the weekend.
2 provided that I have less work to do.
3 so long as it's not on a Sunday.

Conditionals (3) *page 39*

A **A negotiation breakdown**
Specimen answers

If I had been John Dee, I would not have walked out of the discussion. I might have stayed later.

If I had been Mrs Han, I would have made some sort of offer for him to consider as a compromise solution.

B **The credit crunch**

Specimen answer

If I had been in a position to influence events, I would have nationalised Lehman Brothers. I would also have made any bank bailout conditional on appointments to the board of government representatives. I would have introduced legislation to make it illegal to pay bonuses to Wall Street employees until the taxpayers' money had been paid back.

C **Mixed conditionals**

1 a) yes b) yes 2 a) no b) no 3 a) yes b) no 4 a) no b) yes

UNIT 6

Verb combinations (1) *page 41*

A **Verb + verb + *-ing***

1 e 2 a 3 d 4 c 5 b

B **Sentence transformation**

a) I don't mind travelling as long as there are no delays.

b) My job involves meeting many people.

c) I firmly deny passing on any trade secrets.

d) We risk losing business to our competitors.

e) She suggests getting in touch with the commercial attaché.

f) We fully anticipate doubling our turnover in the next two years.

g) He was late so I missed seeing him.

h) How can you justify spending so much on entertainment?

Verb combinations (2) *page 43*

A **Verb + *to*-infinitive**

1 She's promised to do all she can to help.
2 Please remember to send them the samples they requested.
3 We undertake to provide a 24-hour-a-day hotline.
4 I expect to receive an answer soon.
5 They have offered to send a replacement.
6 She neglected to tell them of the potential problem.
7 There appears to be a bug in the program.
8 She claims to have the necessary authority.

B **Verb + object + *to*-infinitive**

1 She taught me to believe in myself.
2 They paid me to do their dirty work.
3 He programmed the robot to perform a certain number of tasks.
4 The employers' federation urged the minister to cut interest rates.
5 The joint venture enabled us to benefit from our partner's expertise.

Verb combinations (3) *page 45*

A **Verbs of perception**

1 moving 2 coming 3 beating 4 being 5 feeling 6 lying 7 whispering
8 going through 9 creeping up

B **Verb patterns**

1 I find **it** impossible to work with him.
2 They made **us work** extremely hard in my previous job.
3 She never let **me take** any decisions.
4 Could you have **Mr Clarke prepare** some statistics?
5 She's finding **it** difficult to get used to the climate.
6 I feel **it** is necessary to delegate more of the work.

Verb combinations (4) *page 47*

A **Verb + *for* + *to*-infinitive**

1 c 2 e 3 b 4 a 5 d

B **Special cases**

1 using 2 to inform 3 going 4 to tell 5 to work; having

UNIT 7

Passives (1) *page 49*

A **Passive verb forms**

1 f 2 d 3 e 4 a 5 b 6 c

B **Focusing on the action**

1 *Das Kapital* was written by Karl Marx.
2 Your car is being repaired now.
3 Apple Computers was founded by Steve Jobs.
4 The proposal will be discussed by the board.
5 Was Mrs Wilson informed?
6 Renault cars are made in Slovenia.
7 He has been transferred to the New York office.
8 The new conference centre was opened by the princess.
9 A full investigation had been made.
10 I didn't realise my telephone conversations were being listened to.

C **Focusing on information**

1 should be read through
2 absorbed
3 a written document needs to be filed
4 can be written on the document
5 a note should be made
6 All messages should be disposed of once they have been dealt with.

Passives (2) *page 51*

A **Check your understanding**

1 false 2 true 3 true 4 false 5 true

B **Active or passive?**

1 are tailored 2 are given 3 are conducted 4 (are) designed 5 encourages 6 build 7 show 8 be saved 9 be used 10 be created 11 help

C **Describing a process**

1 are transported 2 is removed 3 is burnt 4 be generated 5 are cut 6 cooked 7 is bleached 8 remove 9 improve 10 requires 11 are mixed 12 diluted 13 is sprayed 14 is pressed 15 dried 16 wound 17 weighs 18 is controlled 19 correct

UNIT 8

Ability *page 53*

A **Abilities**

1 b 2 f 3 e 4 a 5 g 6 c 7 d

B **Past abilities**

1 managed to 2 could 3 managed to 4 could 5 managed to 6 could 7 could

C **Indicating disapproval**
Specimen answers

1 She could have contacted me on my mobile.
2 She could have let me know.
3 We could have walked.
4 He could have sent me an e-mail.

Obligation, prohibition *page 55*

A **Rules and regulations**
Specimen answers

1 must not 2 have to 3 don't have to 4 must not 5 have to 6 have to 7 have to

B **Rules at work**
Specimen answers

1 must not 2 don't have to 3 have to 4 must not 5 don't have to 6 have to

C **Signs and notices**

1 You have to give way. / You must give way.
2 You must not turn left.
3 You must not overtake.
4 You don't have to change your money into local currency.
5 You must not drive over 30 mph. / You have to drive under 30 mph.
6 You have to be a member to enter.
7 You have to wear protective clothing. / You must not enter.

Possibility *page 57*

A ***can***

Specimen answers

1 Learning a foreign language can often be painful.
2 Entertaining overseas customers can sometimes be hard work.
3 Being in charge of a new project can often be challenging.
4 Setting up in business can occasionally be good fun.
5 Negotiating a contract can sometimes be a waste of time.

B ***could / couldn't***

1 If we diversified, we could offer a wider range of products.
2 If I had stayed in the States, I could have got a better job.
3 In the 1990s you could make a fortune as a 'golden boy'.
4 She could have done an MBA but decided it was too much work.
5 Forty years ago you could buy cigarettes in packets of five.
6 Before privatisation you couldn't buy shares in British Telecom.

C **Missed opportunities**

Specimen answers

He could have become a rock star.

He could have done research at Florida Atlantic University.

He could have become a film star.

He could have sailed in the Admiral's Cup.

Likelihood *page 59*

A **Degrees of likelihood**

1 e 2 b 3 f 4 a 5 d 6 c 7 h 8 g

B **Expressions of likelihood**

may come sooner there is a 67% chance are also likely to produce are not likely to change are highly likely will probably be located

Permission, suggestions, offers *page 61*

A **Permission, suggestions or offers?**

1 S 2 R 3 O 4 R 5 R 6 S 7 O 8 S 9 O

B **Offers and suggestions**

1 We must get together
2 Do you need any help
3 Shall I hold the door open
4 Would you like me
5 I'll give you

Willingness, refusal, promises, threats, typical behaviour *page 63*

A **Uses of *will* and *would***

1 P 2 TB 3 R 4 TB 5 P 6 T 7 P 8 R 9 TB 10 T

B ***will, won't* or *would*?**

1 Accidents **will** happen.
2 **I'll** do my best.
3 She **won't** accept his authority.
4 If you don't pay, legal action **will** be taken.
5 A fanatic is someone who can't change his mind and **won't** change the subject.
6 If you **will** be rude, how can you expect people to like you?
7 He **would** smoke a large cigar before making an important decision.
8 The product with the better-known brand name **will** sell better than the other.

UNIT 9

Types of multi-word verbs *page 65*

A **With or without an object?**

1 – 2 c 3 b 4 e 5 a 6 – 7 – 8 – 9 – 10 d

B **Separable or inseparable?**

1 A 2 A 3 U 4 A 5 A 6 A 7 A 8 U 9 U 10 A 11 U 12 U 13 A 14 A 15 A

Understanding multi-word verbs (1) *page 67*

A **Multi-word verbs with *up***

1 e 2 f 3 b 4 a 5 c 6 d

B **Sentence completion**

1 face up to 2 follow up 3 work up 4 look up 5 pay up 6 play up

C **Sentence completion**

1 save up 2 clear up 3 keep up 4 set up 5 hold ... up 6 think up

Understanding multi-word verbs (2) *page 69*

A Multi-word verbs with *down*

1 break down 2 run down 3 bring down 4 note down 5 cut down 6 play down

B Multi-word verbs with *up*, *down* and *over*

1 e 2 c 3 a 4 b 5 g 6 f 7 d

Understanding multi-word verbs (3) *page 71*

A Particles and their meaning

1

1 e 2 a 3 d 4 c 5 b

2

2 spark off = begin 3 wind up = complete 4 sum up = complete 5 look over = consider
6 note down = write/record 7 keep on = continue 8 back down = admit defeat

B Sentence rearrangement

1 We need to make up for lost time.
2 The firm ran up against strong competition.
3 A number of people have put in for the chairperson's job.
4 They want to back out of the agreement.
5 After a long delay he got round to drafting a reply.
6 Roger thinks he's come up with an answer to our problems.

C A phone conversation

1 put ... through 2 hold on 3 call back 4 tied up 5 get back 6 fix up 7 read ... back

UNIT 10

Adverb position and uses (1) *page 73*

A Sentence rearrangement

1 I am still waiting for confirmation.
2 I never wear jeans at work.
3 He speaks Greek very well.
4 I will probably be able to get it cheaper.
5 I am always pleased to welcome visitors.
6 Her idea is completely absurd.

B Adverb position

Hi! Thanks for your last e-mail. I'm **very** sorry I haven't got back to you sooner but we've been **terribly** rushed in the office. We **always** seem to be extremely busy. It seems the launch has been **remarkably** successful, beyond our wildest dreams in fact. We are **obviously** delighted and we have **already** had a large order from a company in China. This is **absolutely** fabulous news. See you soon.

C **Describing the rate of change**
Specimen answers
Sales of cotton trousers have risen substantially / a great deal / rapidly / sharply.

Sales of casual corduroy trousers have gone up to some extent.

Sales of jeans have risen slightly / gradually / slowly.

Adverb position and uses (2) *page 75*

A **Commenting on the situation**
1 d 2 c 3 e 4 f 5 b 6 a

B **Your situation**
Specimen answers
1 They sometimes arrive late.
2 I usually work in my office.
3 I get on with her very badly.
4 I haven't seen her lately.
5 Quite honestly, I think her performance is awful.

C **Adverb position**
Thank you for the e-mail you sent **yesterday**. I have **already** spoken to Eric but he says he is **still** waiting for confirmation from the board before we can go ahead with the proposed changes. **Quite frankly**, the delay is getting on my nerves but I hope to get started on the project **very soon**. As is **often** the case, we will **suddenly** receive confirmation at the last minute and have to work **flat out** for the next couple of months in order to get into production **fast**.

UNIT 11

Noun formation *page 77*

A **Noun formation**
acceptance
agreement
counterfeiting
entry / entrance
initiation
occurrence
protection
racism / racist
reference
storage
wastage
awareness
complexity
creativity / creation
effectiveness
prosperity
punctuality
reality / realism
reliability
socialism / society
weakness
wisdom

B **Activities**
1 f 2 c 3 a 4 e 5 b 6 d

C **People**

1 receptionist 2 employee 3 lawyer 4 auditor / accountant 5 estate agent / realtor 6 electrician 7 reporter / journalist 8 photographer 9 applicants / candidates

Types of noun *page 79*

A **Countable or uncountable?**

1 U 2 C 3 C 4 U 5 C 6 U 7 C 8 U 9 C 10 U 11 U 12 C

B **Matching countable and uncountable nouns**

Countable	*Uncountable*
cars	traffic
machines	equipment
policies	insurance
accidents	damage
jobs	employment
journey	travel
hints	advice
bulletins	news
laws	legislation

Plural nouns *page 81*

A **Nouns only occurring in the plural**

1 outskirts 2 means 3 valuables 4 goods 5 premises 6 works 7 Refreshments 8 crossroads

B **Making nouns plural**

1 bags 2 people 3 parties 4 formulas / formulae 5 potatoes 6 shelves 7 faxes 8 knives 9 criteria 10 matches

C **Singular or plural?**

1 is 2 have 3 are 4 are 5 is 6 has / have

D **Common mistakes**

1 The news **is** bad, I'm afraid.
2 She knows a great many **people**.
3 Stress at work is not a recent **phenomenon**.
4 Our office is situated **in pleasant surroundings**.
5 The **staff** are unhappy with the new arrangements.

Two nouns together *page 83*

A **Famous places**

Berlin's Brandenburg Gate Venice's canals Madrid's Prado London's Big Ben New York's skyscrapers Cairo's pyramids

B **Amounts and quantities**

1 f 2 c 3 a 4 e 5 d 6 b

C **Noun + *of* + noun**

1 basket of currencies 2 breach of contract 3 rate of return 4 conflict of interest 5 letter of credit

Compound nouns *page 85*

A **Noun combinations**

1 sales 2 account 3 market 4 brand 5 trade

B **Choice of structures**

1 ✓ 2 ✗ 3 ✗ 4 ✓ 5 ✓ 6 ✗ 7 ✓ 8 ✗ 9 ✓ 10 ✗ 11 ✓ 12 ✓ 13 ✗ 14 ✓ 15 ✗ 16 ✗ 17 ✗ 18 ✓

C **Compound nouns**

1 production 2 figures 3 sense 4 loyalty 5 revenue

Nouns and prepositions *page 87*

A **Which preposition?**

1 in 2 in 3 of 4 for 5 on 6 for 7 to 8 under

B **Prepositional phrases**

1 beyond 2 by 3 in 4 on 5 at

UNIT 12

Articles (*a*/*an*, *the* and zero article) *page 89*

A ***a*/*an*, *the* and zero article**

1 (Cambridge) Category 13
2 (job) Category 6
3 (clocks) Category 12
4 (idea) Category 1
5 (CBI) Category 9
6 (people) Category 12
7 (course) Category 1
8 (loan) Category 1
9 (business) Category 1
10 (school) Category 5
11 (children) Category 6
12 (unemployed) Category 8
13 (information) Category 11
14 (sources) Category 12
15 (advice) Category 11
16 (accountant) Category 2
17 (village) Category 5/6
18 (trade) Category 8
19 (month) Category 3
20 (thing) Category 10

B **Ferrari**

1 a 2 the 3 the 4 the 5 a 6 The 7 the 8 a 9 Ø 10 Ø 11 Ø 12 the 13 the 14 Ø 15 the 16 the 17 The 18 a 19 the 20 the 21 the

Quantifiers (1) *page 91*

A **Amounts**

1 any 2 no 3 some 4 Some 5 None 6 some 7 any 8 no; any 9 some
10 any; none 11 any 12 Some

B **A letter of complaint**

1 none 2 any 3 no 4 some 5 all 6 any 7 no

Quantifiers (2) *page 93*

A **Correct the errors**

1 He didn't reply **fast enough**.
2 The flood caused **a lot of** damage.
3 What she said was a **little** strange.
4 The whole process uses very **little** electricity.
5 I enjoyed **a** few of her books but not all of them.
6 We haven't made **much** / **a lot of** progress recently.
7 I don't think he has **enough experience** for the job.
8 She works mostly on her own so she has very **few** colleagues.
9 I've got **a** few minutes to spare so we can continue if you like.
10 The final date for submission was three weeks ago so it's far **too** late now.

B **An e-mail**

1 a little 2 few 3 much 4 little 5 few 6 many 7 too 8 a great deal
9 a few 10 enough

UNIT 13

Adjectives *page 95*

A **Your personal profile**

Individual responses

B **Adjective formation**

1 successful 2 scientific 3 competitive 4 responsible 5 promotional 6 autonomous
7 accurate 8 technical 9 competent 10 loyal

Compound adjectives *page 97*

A **Compound adjectives**

1 free 2 self 3 minded 4 well 5 term 6 high

B **Adjectives and nouns**

1 e 2 d 3 g 4 c 5 h 6 b 7 f 8 a

1 stiff competition 2 joint account 3 heated exchange 4 high priority 5 last resort
6 stumbling block 7 foregone conclusion 8 vested interest

Adjective position *page 99*

A **Which adjective?**

1 former 2 last 3 previous 4 present 5 major 6 obvious

B **Before or after the noun?**

1 issues discussed 2 money allocated 3 points raised 4 uniform issued 5 goods ordered
6 women questioned 7 outstanding ability 8 involved argument

C **Sentence rearrangement**

1 The statement issued by the government was misinterpreted.

2 The problems raised during the meeting have been solved.

3 The main thing is that you shouldn't worry.

4 Her refusal to cooperate has put me in an impossible situation.

Adjectives and adverbs *page 101*

A **Common mistakes**

1 ✓

2 I work **hard** because I am highly paid.

3 ✓

4 Everything I do recently seems to go **wrong**.

5 We need to start **early**.

6 ✓

7 Time is running **short**.

B **Adverb position**

1 extremely 2 increasingly 3 unfortunately 4 deeply 5 awfully 6 suitably 7 easily
8 hugely

Prepositions of place and direction *page 103*

A **Which preposition?**

1 in 2 across 3 (a)round 4 at / by 5 through 6 beyond 7 from 8 to

B **Sentence completion**

1 around / about 2 from 3 in 4 on 5 from; (a)round 6 through; from; to 7 by 8 in; to
9 down / up / across 10 beyond

Prepositions of time *page 105*

A **Which preposition?**

1 on 2 in 3 through 4 at; on 5 in 6 from; to 7 in 8 beyond 9 by 10 around

B **Prepositions of time**
Specimen answers

He's leaving tomorrow on flight BA 515 to Paris and staying at the Hotel du Nord.

On 4 May he's meeting Monsieur Vatel at 22 rue Danton.

The following day there's a board meeting from 10 o'clock to 12.30.

The phone bill must be paid by 7 May.

Jane's coming back from Dublin around 11.30 on 7 May.

On 8 May he has to pick Lucy up from her dance lesson at 5pm.

On 8 May the new share option scheme comes into force.

On 9 May there'll be a dinner party for Bill's birthday from 8pm until midnight.

UNIT 14

Advising *page 107*

A **Giving advice**

1 You'd better hurry, or you'll miss the plane.
2 My advice would be to sell your shares now.
3 Don't drive through the city centre during rush hour.
4 You'd better see a doctor if you're feeling ill.
5 You'd better not tell her the bad news yet.
6 If I were you, I'd declare my overseas investments to the tax authorities.
7 It's worth asking for a second opinion.

B **If I were you, ...**
Specimen answer

My advice would be to keep Mr Mudd in Customer Relations as he is unlikely to be of much use elsewhere. In my opinion, his salary should now be frozen unless he agrees to take on more responsibility to justify his higher salary.

Agreeing and disagreeing *page 109*

A ***so / neither***

1 Neither did I. 2 Neither can I. 3 So should I. 4 Neither have I. 5 So do I. 6 So do I.

B **Shades of opinion**

Specimen answers

1 All men and women should do military service.

I disagree with that completely.

2 There should be a single world currency.

Yes, but you still have to remember that people are attached to their currencies.

3 National industries should be protected.

Yes, I'd go along with that up to a point but you can't ignore market forces entirely.

4 Bonuses are perfectly acceptable forms of remuneration.

Performance bonuses, up to a certain financial limit, are a perfectly acceptable form of remuneration as long as they are awarded on objective criteria and seen by all to have been distributed to those who deserve them.

5 Men and women should retire at 55.

You may have a point but what about the social security deficit?

Asking for information *page 111*

A **Asking questions**

2 Are 3 Where 4 How old 5 What 6 How long 7 How much 8 How often 9 When 10 Why 11 Which

B **A bad line**

1 How many people visited 2 Who congratulated 3 Who / Which director

Comparing products and services *page 113*

A **Making comparisons**

1 b 2 d 3 f 4 a 5 g 6 h 7 e 8 c

B **Common mistakes**

1 Lisbon is not as big **as** London.

2 There is more to life **than** a spreadsheet.

3 The disadvantage of this project is that it is not as cheap **as** the other.

4 Women's pay is **much** lower than men's, even for the same work.

5 Metro is the world's second **biggest** retailer after Wal-Mart Stores of the US.

C **Global MBA rankings**

1 the highest 2 The most significant 3 more than 4 closest 5 compared with 6 much more 7 much faster 8 more or less the same

Complaining and apologising *page 115*

A **A letter of complaint**

1 I will have no alternative but to 2 I am writing to express my concern 3 Regrettably,

The order of the letter is as follows:

Dear Mrs O'Malley,
I am writing to express my concern ...
Regrettably, this delay ...
Given the long-standing relationship ...
However, if the delay continues, ...
I look forward to ...
Yours sincerely,

B **A letter of apology**

1 We are very concerned
2 We very much regret
3 I assure you we are doing everything in our power
4 Once again, we apologise
5 hope you will understand the reason

Confirming information *page 117*

A **Confirming decisions**

1 wasn't she 2 didn't she 3 didn't he 4 did he 5 would it 6 didn't we
7 shouldn't we 8 isn't it 9 hadn't we 10 shall we

B **A conversation at a cocktail party**

1 aren't you? 2 weren't you? 3 isn't it? 4 haven't you? 5 shall I?

Describing a company *page 119*

A **HMV**

1 consists of 2 the world's foremost 3 leading 4 operates 5 worldwide

B **Wieden+Kennedy**

1 world-class 2 headquartered 3 operations 4 range 5 headquarters 6 located 7 employs

C **Sita**

Specimen answer

Based in Geneva, SITA is a major player in the field of telecommunications and ranks No. 1 for the number of connections worldwide. We are present in 220 countries with over 900 separate locations generating a revenue of $1.42 billion and employing 3,400 people.

Describing processes *page 121*

A **Active or passive?**

1 integrates 2 relies 3 is coordinated 4 ensures 5 is managed 6 be synthesised 7 be scheduled 8 is given 9 are checked 10 be used 11 been met 12 be warehoused 13 been fulfilled 14 are given 15 is built up 16 be located 17 be limited

Describing trends *page 123*

A **Trends in consumer relationships**

1 has changed (the change is described as complete)
2 have never seen
3 has replaced
4 have never had
5 have realised / have been realising (the change is still under way, although some companies may have become fully aware of the change)
6 has been based
7 have been re-examining
8 have taken / have been taking
9 has become

B **Describing trends**
Specimen answers

Trends in overall online travel market size
More and more people are booking their holidays online. From 1998 until 2003 the upward trend was relatively slow but from 2004 we have seen increases of 10 billion euros per annum. All in all, over a ten-year period, sales went up from just 0.2 bn euros to almost 50 bn euros and the trend is expected to continue.

Retail sales trends
Over the last twelve months retail sales have seen many ups and downs. After an encouraging start to the year – in January sales were up by 8% compared to the previous year – consumer spending went into decline from February until June when it was 6 percentage points down on the year before. Sales picked up over the next three months but fell back in September. Since then, sales have rallied, no doubt owing to the traditional Christmas rush.

Forecasting and speculating *page 125*

A **Forecasting**
Specimen answers

1 I'm likely to get a pay rise soon.
2 My firm is unlikely to be taken over.
3 I'm very unlikely to be made redundant.
4 I'm bound to get promoted.
5 There is bound to be a change of government in the next six months.

B **Speculating**

1 b) can't 2 a) must 3 e) can't 4 f) must 5 d) must 6 c) can't

C **Making hypotheses**

Specimen answers

1 The director must have had inside knowledge.

2 The employees must have got food poisoning.

3 He can't have spoken to her in Urdu.

4 He must have been embezzling the money.

Getting things done *page 127*

A **Getting things done**

1 We get / have all our export risks insured.

2 I have my car serviced by the garage every 15,000 kilometres.

3 We get a specialist agency to translate all the company documentation and manuals.
We get / have all the company documentation and manuals translated by a specialist agency.

4 We're having a new extension built by the contractors.
We're having the contractors build a new extension.

5 I had the contract drawn up by the legal department.
I had the legal department draw up the contract.

B **Arranging for things to be done**

1 We need to get / have the printer fixed.

2 We'll need to get / have her replaced.

3 I need to get / have them cleaned.

4 I need to get / have them checked.

Giving instructions *page 129*

A **Changing a wheel**

1 Park the car on a flat, stable surface and apply the handbrake firmly. (C)

2 Raise the vehicle off the ground with a jack. (G)

3 Prise out the centre hub cap. (A)

4 Unscrew the wheel bolts. (E)

5 Remove the wheel and replace it with the spare. (F)

6 Tighten the wheel bolts. (H)

7 Replace the centre hub cap. (D)

8 Lower the vehicle and remove the jack. (B)

B Giving directions

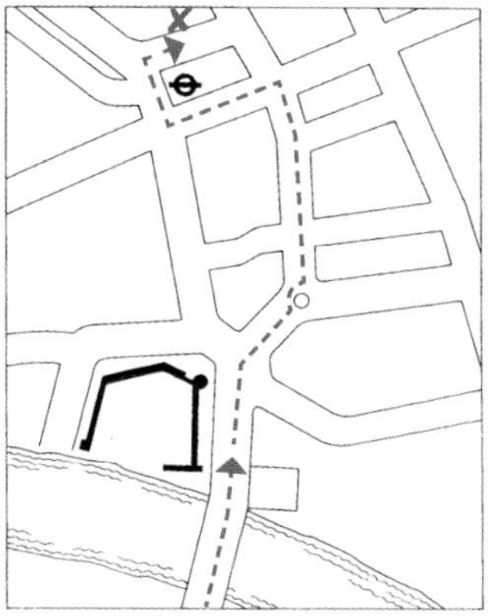

Planning ahead *page 131*

A **Making arrangements**
Specimen answers

1 Who is going to print the programme? How many copies will you be needing?
2 How will the delegates be getting from the airport to the hotel?
3 What are they going to do in the evening? / What kind of entertainment are you planning to put on?
4 Who will be making the opening address?
5 What are you planning for / to do after dinner on Monday evening?
6 Which room will you be holding the plenary session in?
7 What will Rod Weir be talking about?
8 What do you intend to provide for vegetarians?
9 How many rooms will you be needing for the workshops?
10 What size rooms are you going to use?
11 What equipment will you be needing?
12 What time will the delegates be going back to the airport?

Reporting what people say or think (1) *page 133*

A **Reporting what the MD said**

1 He said (that) he thought a joint venture was the best way to break into the Middle East.
2 He said (that) he was / we were not planning to set up a subsidiary.
3 He said (that) he / we had been talking to a group of investors in the Gulf.
4 He said (that) he'd talked to the commercial attaché at the embassy.
5 He said (that) he didn't want to diversify in the immediate future.
6 He said (that) we shouldn't attempt to move too fast because we might get our fingers burnt.
7 He said (that) he / we would be sending Stuart Campbell on a fact-finding mission.

B **News in brief**
1 e 2 c 3 a 4 b 5 d

Reporting what people say or think (2) *page 135*

A **The minutes of a meeting**
1 raised 2 invited 3 outlined 4 acknowledged 5 reminded 6 pointed out 7 disagreed 8 advised 9 complained 10 confirmed 11 suggested 12 offered 13 warned

Reporting questions *page 137*

A **Sentence transformation**
2 He / She asked me if I had seen Bernard yet.
3 Could you tell me if you are open on a Saturday?
4 He / She wondered if / whether I had got his message.
5 Have you any idea how much time there is left?
6 He / She wanted to know if / whether she would be taking her husband with her.

B **Enquiries**
2 Someone asked her where you can get a shuttle (from).
3 Someone asked her where you can get foreign currency.
4 Someone asked her where the duty free was.
5 Someone asked her where they could leave their suitcases.
6 Someone asked her why the Lufthansa flight had been delayed.

Requesting and offering *page 139*

A **Polite requests**
Specimen answers
1 Do you mind if I leave early?
I'm sorry, you can't. This meeting is very important.
2 Shall I give you a lift?
That's very kind of you.
3 I was wondering if you could lend me $50 until tomorrow.
Well, I'm afraid I haven't got any money.
4 Would you like a glass of sherry?
No, thanks. I don't drink sherry.
5 Could I have the bill, please?
Certainly.
6 Could you tell me the way to the station, please?
I'm afraid I don't know where it is.

B **Doing someone a favour**

1 I'm afraid 2 Shall I 3 go ahead 4 I was wondering if 5 I'll 6 could you possibly

A Could I ask you a favour?
B Yeah, go ahead.
A I was wondering if you could phone these people in Spain for me. My Spanish is atrocious.
B No problem. Just tell me what you want me to say.
A Shall I write it down for you?
B Yes. Otherwise I'll forget! When do you want me to phone them?
A Tomorrow.
B Well, I'm afraid I can't tomorrow. I'm not coming in to the office.
A Well, could you possibly do it the day after tomorrow?
B Sure. I'll do it first thing.

Suggesting *page 141*

A **Making suggestions**

1 b How about hiring a new public relations manager?
2 e How about offering her some kind of promotion to a more highly-paid position?
3 a Shall we stay in a nearby hotel overnight?
4 c Well, I suggest taking them to a night club.
5 d We could give people more responsibility for decision-making.

B **Problem-solving**
Specimen answers

1 I suggest that we should review our internal promotion policy.
2 Why don't we use a factoring agency?
3 Shouldn't we offer a bigger discount?
4 You could sell them at reduced prices to the employees and their families.
5 I think you should do what you can reasonably do in work time and leave the rest.

Understanding signs and notices *page 143*

A **Signs and notices**

1 c 2 a 3 b 4 c 5 i 6 d 7 e 8 f 9 h 10 g 11 g 12 b 13 a

UNIT 15

Adding and combining information *page 145*

A **Definitions: a financial quiz**

1 e) where 2 d) that / which 3 f) whose 4 b) who 5 g) that / which 6 c) who 7 a) where

B ***whose, who, which, that***
1 whose 2 who 3 which 4 whose 5 that / which 6 that / which

Emphasising *page 147*

A **Ajaz Ahmed**
1 truly 2 to say the least 3 whole 4 whatsoever 5 total 6 Indeed 7 so 8 such

Expressing a reaction *page 149*

A **Indicating attitude**
1 understandably 2 Paradoxically 3 typically 4 mysteriously 5 conveniently

B **Exclamations**

1
1 How
2 What a
3 What
4 How
5 What a
6 How
7 How

2
1 What a mess!
2 How extravagant!
3 How disgusting!
4 How lucky!
5 What rubbish!
6 How awful!
7 What a fantastic idea!

Generalising / Indicating relevance *page 151*

A **General statements**
1 and large 2 in all 3 the whole 4 a rule 5 general

B **... speaking**
1 Aesthetically speaking 2 Broadly speaking 3 Technically speaking 4 relatively speaking

C **Points of view**
1 d 2 a 3 e 4 b 5 c

Highlighting information *page 153*

A **Highlighting information**
1 f 2 b 3 a 4 e 5 d 6 c

B **Focusing on the topic**

1

a) What we need is a good overseas partner.

b) What you have to have is the right distribution network.

c) What you must do is make sure your products are suited to the local market.

2

a) What I will do then is describe the project in more detail.

b) What I will do next is tell you how we defined the potential market.

c) What I want to do is convince you that this project is worth investing in.

C **Negative ideas**

1 Never have we faced such a difficult challenge.

2 Under no circumstances should you handle dangerous products without protective clothing.

3 On no account must you tell him about our plans.

Linking (1) *page 155*

A **Contrasting**

1 Despite 2 Although 3 Yet 4 Although 5 Nevertheless 6 Whereas

B **Link words**

1 Although 2 However 3 Despite 4 whereas

Linking (2) *page 157*

A **Categories of link words**

Contrast	*Result*	*Extra information*	*Sequencing in time*
on the other hand	consequently	moreover	formerly
alternatively	so	also	meanwhile
even so	thus	too	subsequently
nevertheless	therefore	furthermore	eventually

B **Link the statements**

1 b 2 e 3 a 4 c 5 f 6 d

Substituting *page 159*

A ***so* and *not***

1 Yes, I expect so. 2 Yes, I imagine so. 3 Yes, I guess so. 4 No, I'm afraid not.
5 No, I hope not. 6 No, I suppose not.

B **Avoiding repetition**

1 I may be free this afternoon. If so, I'll come and see you.

2 Africa has long had a bad reputation for business – companies investing there fear the unknown, and often rightly so.

3 A senior monetary official said that he regretted the decision not to join the EMU in 1999 for one particular reason: the operational structure of the Bank of England would have made a perfect role model for the European Central Bank – much more so than the German Bundesbank.

C **Referring**

so = spilt coffee onto the laptop, trodden on it or dropped it

this = damaging a laptop

those = fully-ruggedised laptops

the latter = rubber corner 'bumpers'

Such = the engineering that makes laptops suitable for physically challenging environments

These = business-rugged laptops

These machines = machines that are sturdy and relatively accident-proof

UNIT 16

Managing a conversation (1) *page 161*

A **Introducing a topic**
Specimen answers

1 Have you heard that Christine is leaving?

2 Did you go to the performance of *The Magic Flute*?

3 Have you heard about the latest developments?

4 Did you hear about the disaster in the planning department?

B **Changing a topic**
Specimen answers

1 By the way, did he arrange for overtime at the weekend?

2 While we're on the subject of China, did you hear what happened in Beijing?

3 This is on a completely different subject, but Sandra wants to move into another section.

C **Echoing**
Conversation 1

A And if you book before the end of the month you get a 10% reduction.

B Before the end of the month?

A Yeah, that's what it said on the leaflet.

Conversation 2

C Well, I thought there was something wrong with the system.

D Something wrong?

C Yeah, but it was working all right in the morning.

Managing a conversation (2) *page 163*

A **Keeping going**

1 or something 2 a bit like 3 as I was saying 4 anyway

B **Conversational acts**

1 d 2 a 3 e 4 b 5 c

Negotiating *page 165*

A **Negotiating an agreement**

1 d 2 b 3 c 4 a

Presenting figures *page 167*

A **Saying figures aloud**

1 oh/zero/nought point four five
2 one point eight five
3 seven hundred fifty-nine dollars (US) / seven hundred and fifty-nine dollars (UK)
4 a/one hundred and twenty-five million yen
5 a third / one-third
6 two-fifths
7 one in three; a ratio of one to three
8 two thousand and one
9 three four two five four six one
10 three seven four nine

B **In your situation?**

Specimen answers

1 About 10% of my time is spent in leisure activities.
2 On average, 2.2 children are born to each couple.
3 It's in the region of the equivalent of £35,000 a year.
4 It's 3.75%.
5 It's about 3%.
6 One in three employees is a woman.

Presenting information *page 169*

A **Presenting a company**

1 I'd like first of all to give you an overview
2 First
3 second
4 third
5 As you can see from the slide,
6 And to complete the picture
7 Now I would like to describe
8 If you look at
9 Then
10 So, to recapitulate

Presenting visual information *page 172*

A **Illustrations**

1 flow chart 2 graph 3 pie chart 4 bar chart 5 table 6 diagram 7 vertical axis 8 horizontal axis 9 curve 10 dotted line

B **Describing graphs**

1

1 at 2 from 3 of 4 under 5 of 6 by 7 to

2

Specimen answers

Fewer jobs, higher pay

Average real wages in Germany declined by more than 3% between 2000 and 2004 but rose again over the next two years by 1%. They dipped in the following year but by 2009 had gone back to the same level as in 2001.

During the same period, unemployment also fluctuated. In 2005 it stood at just under 12% of the working population. However, the job market recovered steadily, standing at about 8% in 2009.

Consumer comeback

As a percentage of GDP, Chinese exports rose steadily by 20% between 2000 and 2007 before going down slightly over the next two years.

At the same time private consumption fell by ten percentage points before levelling off as from 2006.

Volatile prices

Between 2000 and 2009 the rate of inflation in Libya fluctuated wildly. It slumped from 10% to nearly zero at the beginning of the decade before rising again to its previous level in 2003. Over the next four years it zig-zagged between 10 and 15% before rocketting to over 25% in 2008, then slumping back the following year to its rate in 2007.

Social interaction *page 175*

A **Reacting to what people say**

1 You're joking! 2 I didn't quite catch that. 3 How come? 4 Never mind. 5 Oh dear!

a) How come? b) Never mind. c) You're joking! d) Oh dear! e) I didn't quite catch that.

B **Conversational pairs**

1 i 2 g 3 h 4 b 5 f 6 a 7 j 8 c 9 d 10 e

Taking part in meetings *page 177*

A **Chairing a meeting**

1 d 2 g 3 h 4 a 5 f 6 e 7 c 8 b

B **Taking part in a meeting**

1 f 2 e 3 a 4 c 5 d 6 b

Telephoning *page 179*

A **A phone conversation**

2 Hello. My name's Beata Szlachetka. I'd like to speak to Katie Chapman, please.
3 Sorry, I didn't quite catch that.
4 Beata Szlachetka and I'd like to speak to Katie Chapman.
5 Hold the line, please. I'll see if she's in.
6 (pause) Hello. Katie Chapman speaking.
7 Hello. This is Beata.
8 Hi, Beata. How are you doing?
9 Fine, thanks. And you?
10 OK. Busy as usual.
11 I'm just ringing to find out if you've received the copies of the contract.
12 Yeah, they came this morning but I haven't signed them yet.
13 OK, there's no rush.
14 I'll sign them this afternoon and send them back to you.
15 Great. Thanks a lot.

B **Telephone language**

Numbers 7 and 8 are recorded messages.

C **Taking someone's name**

1 Graham Hughes
2 Janice Young

The language of contracts *page 181*

A **A contract**

1 Parties
2 WHEREAS
3 terms and conditions
4 set forth
5 covenant
6 said
7 shall
8 terms
9 forthwith
10 breach
11 construed

Index

The first number refers to the page number. The second number refers to the number of the entry on that page. For example:

articles 88 means that you can read about articles on page 88.

going to 28,2; 28,3; 132,2 means you can read about the uses of *going to* on page 28 (sections 2 and 3) and on page 132 (section 2).

B

C

D

P